# Overcoming Anxiety and **Depression** on the **Autism Spectrum**

## A Self-Help Guide Using CBT

# Lee A. Wilkinson, PhD

Jessica Kingsley *Publishers*
London and Philadelphia

Figure 3.1 'E–S Scores and Cognitive Styles' on page 34; Appendix A 'The Adult Autism Spectrum Quotient (AQ) Test' on pages 103–108; Appendix B 'The Adult Empathy Quotient (EQ) Test' on pages 109–115; and Appendix C 'The Adult Systematizing Quotient (SQ) Test on pages 117–123 are reproduced with kind permission of the Journal of Autism and Developmental Disorders.

First published in 2015
by Jessica Kingsley Publishers
73 Collier Street
London N1 9BE, UK
and
400 Market Street, Suite 400
Philadelphia, PA 19106, USA

*www.jkp.com*

**Library of Congress Cataloging in Publication Data**
Wilkinson, Lee A. (Lee Anthony)
  Overcoming anxiety and depression on the autism spectrum : a self-help guide using CBT / Lee A.
Wilkinson.
    pages cm
  Includes bibliographical references.
  ISBN 978-1-84905-927-5 (alk. paper)
  1. Autism spectrum disorders--Patients--Rehabilitation. 2. Autism spectrum disorders--Patients--
Mental health. 3. Cognitive therapy. 4. Anxiety--Treatment. 5. Depression, Mental--Treatment. 6. Self-
help techniques.  I. Title.
  RC553.A88W53 2015
  616.85'882--dc23
                            2014026828

**British Library Cataloguing in Publication Data**
A CIP catalogue record for this book is available from the British Library

ISBN 978 1 84905 927 5
eISBN 978 0 85700 710 0

Printed and bound in Great Britain
By Bell and Bain Ltd, Glasgow

*To the memory of my parents,*
*Lee C. and Anna M. Wilkinson*

# ACKNOWLEDGMENTS

This book represents a combination of many years of practice as a psychologist and autism professional. I would like to take this opportunity to extend my gratitude to the children and youth with whom I have worked over the years, their families and others in the autism community. Without you, this book would not have been written. I also extend my appreciation to the editorial staff at Jessica Kingsley Publishers. Special thanks to Rachel Menzies, for her assistance in bringing the project forward, and to Kate Mason, for her skillful work in editing the manuscript. As always, I am most grateful to my spouse, Amy, for her patience, support, and encouragement during the writing process.

# CONTENTS

# CHAPTER 1

# INTRODUCTION

## Adults on the Autism Spectrum

The dramatic increase in the prevalence of autism spectrum conditions among children and adolescents and the correspondingly large number of youth transitioning into adulthood has created an urgent need to address the problems faced by many adults on the autism spectrum. There is no adult-onset autism spectrum condition. Symptoms have generally been present in childhood and extend into adulthood. Although adolescence and early adulthood may bring about some symptom reduction and improved functioning, we now know that autism is a continuous and lifelong condition and that individuals seldom move off the autism spectrum (Holmboe *et al.*, 2014). Similarly, autistic traits have been found to be highly stable when measured in the general (typical) population. It seems quite clear that rather than outgrowing their symptoms, children with autism spectrum conditions become adults with autism spectrum conditions (Seltzer *et al.*, 2004; Shea and Mesibov, 2005; Wilkinson, 2008). Moreover, there is a large and heterogeneous group of adults whose autistic traits were not identified in childhood and therefore may not have received the appropriate interventions and supports. As a result, there are a significant number of adults who are now seeking help to deal with feelings of social isolation, interpersonal difficulties, anxiety, depressed mood, and coping problems often associated with being situated on the autism spectrum. It is only recently that mental health professionals have begun to appreciate the complex challenges faced by a lost generation of adults who are now an underserved population (Wilkinson, 2007). The focus of intervention must shift from remediating the core symptoms of childhood to promoting adaptive behaviors that can facilitate quality of life and psychological well-being in adulthood (Orsmond *et al.*, 2013).

While there is no shortage of books describing the controversies and challenges related to the diagnosis and treatment of autism spectrum conditions, there is a need for a practical resource for adults on the spectrum that promotes self-understanding and directly teaches effective ways of coping with their emotional challenges. This self-help guide provides a different way of looking at adult autism spectrum conditions and addresses the discomfort that many individuals experience deviating from what is generally referred to as "neurotypicality." It provides a rational approach to managing anxiety and depression and is intended to help the individual find their own space and feel comfortable with themselves. It does not focus on a specific or single autism-related condition (e.g. Asperger syndrome), nor is it intended to confirm or sanction a diagnosis or help establish a self-identity. The primary objective of this book is to provide a self-help resource that will lead to greater self-understanding, self-advocacy, and better decision-making in life span activities such as employment and interpersonal relationships for adults on the autism spectrum. It is written from a positive and strength-based perspective. The intended audience is individuals in the early and middle years of adulthood, with and without a formal diagnosis, who share features associated with autism spectrum conditions. This includes adults who may have achieved an optimal outcome and no longer meet the criteria for a diagnosis, but who continue to experience subtle deficits in communication and social adaptive behavior. It is also appropriate for adults who recognize their autistic traits, even though they may not have experienced major social difficulties and clinical impairment, but who want to improve their emotional well-being.

## Cognitive Behavioral Therapy (CBT)

The activities and procedures described in this book fall under the umbrella label of Cognitive Behavioral Therapy (CBT). CBT has direct applicability to adults on the autism spectrum who often have difficulty understanding, managing, and expressing emotions (Attwood, 2004, 2006; Cardaciotto and Herbert, 2004; Gaus, 2011; Hare, 1997; Scattone and Mong, 2013). It has been shown to be effective in changing the way a person thinks about and responds to feelings such as anxiety and depression (Beck *et al.*, 1979; Epp and Dobson, 2010). Although there are a variety of CBT approaches, most share some common elements and objectives. Among the primary goals of CBT are to identify and challenge dysfunctional/unrealistic beliefs, cognitions or thoughts. Through CBT, the individual learns skills to modify thoughts and beliefs through a variety of techniques and strategies to improve interaction with others in effective and appropriate ways, thereby promoting self-regulation and improving mental health. It is a goal-oriented approach and primarily emphasizes here-and-now problems, regardless of one's past history, traits, or diagnosis (Dobson and Dozois, 2010).

CBT, by definition, teaches people to monitor their own thoughts, ideas, and perceptions with the goal of becoming more aware of their interpretive errors. CBT builds a set of skills that enables an individual to be aware of thoughts and emotions; identify how situations, thoughts, and behaviors influence emotions; and improve feelings by changing dysfunctional thoughts and behaviors. It shows you how you are now creating your present emotional and behavioral problems rather than encouraging you to understand and explain how events in your past or how being on the autism spectrum are the reasons for your upsets. It provides you with practical, action-oriented exercises  that will help you work and practice new ways of thinking and behaving. CBT also shows how to use rational thinking for self-control and to manage your own emotional well-being. Finally, it shows you how to be a clear-thinking individual who accepts him or herself, but at the same time lives successfully and comfortably in a challenging social world.

The basic principle of CBT is that we mainly feel the way we think and that anxiety and depression originate in our irrational beliefs or cognitive distortions (DeRubeis *et al.*, 2010; Dryden, David, and Ellis, 2010). In other words, illogical and unrealistic thinking can lead to feelings of anxiety and depression and affect your psychological well-being. This book will teach you to identify and modify the irrational beliefs and cognitive distortions that are causing these problems without changing who you are. Rather that focusing on changing your autistic traits, you will learn how to change your beliefs about how they affect your emotional well-being. This means (a) learning new cognitive and behavioral skills; (b) learning coping and compensatory strategies for problems that cannot be changed; and (c) learning self-acceptance and remaining uniquely you.

The majority of behavioral change is usually achieved outside of therapy and in our day-to-day lives. CBT has often been described as guided self-help, and this self-help book will help you learn how CBT can help you overcome your anxiety and depression. It takes the best of the techniques and procedures from the widely practiced, evidenced-based CBT models of cognitive therapy (CT) and rational-emotive-behavior therapy (REBT) and adapts them so that they can be used by the average person in real-world situations (DeRubeis *et al.*, 2010; Dryden *et al.*, 2010). This guide will help you gain some useful insights and begin to work through your problems without a therapist or mental health professional. In effect, you become your own therapist by understanding and managing your own thinking (cognitive), feeling (emotional), and acting (behavior), in order to improve your psychological well-being. It will help you to uncover and identify basic unrealistic ideas and by using rational thinking, change the notions which underlie and create your feelings of anxiety and depression. You will also learn how to self-analyze and observe your own feelings and actions, and how to evaluate them objectively. CBT differs from traditional talking therapeutic approaches in that it uses a psychoeducational approach to teach the person how to apply methods and techniques to their problems. Consequently, you will find this book to be directive rather than reflective in its approach.

## Organization of this book

Although this book avoids categorizing or labeling individuals, it does provide you with an opportunity to engage in self-analysis and discover where you are situated on the spectrum. It will also facilitate self-awareness, self-acceptance, and promote adaptive behaviors that can lead to a greater sense of satisfaction and fulfillment in your everyday life. Chapter 2 includes a discussion of condition versus disorder and summarizes the emotional problems that frequently co-occur with autism spectrum conditions. You will learn that autistic traits are continuously distributed in the general (normal) population and that "we all have some autistic traits." Chapter 3 discusses self-analysis versus diagnosis (and self-diagnosis). It describes how the weak central coherence and empathizing-systemizing (E–S) theories can help explain your autistic traits. Self-report questionnaires are used to illustrate both the social and non-social features of autism spectrum conditions. You will have an opportunity to determine your cognitive and emotional style (different ways of learning, feeling, and thinking). Chapter 4 introduces you to the basic principle of CBT, the ABC theory of emotions (feelings). You will discover that it is not the situation or event that directly causes you to become upset, but rather how you think about, view, or interpret it that creates your negative emotional consequence or disturbed feelings. You will also learn to identify some common unhelpful thinking habits and to see the "bigger picture." Chapter 5 examines the common cognitive distortions and irrational thoughts (beliefs) which can lead to anxiety and depression. Major irrational beliefs and rational alternative beliefs are presented and reviewed. This chapter teaches you how to think scientifically, utilize disputing as an intervention to challenge your irrational and unrealistic beliefs, and substitute them with rational/functional and appropriate feelings and behaviors. You will learn to distinguish between feeling appropriately concerned, frustrated, sad, apprehensive, or annoyed and inappropriately depressed, anxious, or angry. You will come to understand that regardless of background, personal history, or where you are situated on the autism spectrum, you have the capacity for self-awareness and can control your own emotional destiny. The chapter concludes with a discussion of self-acceptance and perfectionism. Chapter 6 describes some additional CBT techniques. You will learn how imagery, mindfulness, self-talk, and problem-solving strategies can be used to help you cope with your emotional upsets. Chapter 7 concludes with a brief summary of the key points and insights of CBT and how to cope with relapse and maintain your emotional gains. It is important to note that the chapters of this book were designed to be read in the order presented. You are urged to attend carefully to the chapter on the ABCs of Emotions. Likewise, it is especially important to complete the exercises and activities in each chapter, and utilize the worksheets and forms in the book's appendix. (Appendices F to I can also be downloaded from the JKP website at www.jkp.com/overcoming-anxiety-and-depression-on-the-autism-spectrum.html).

As with any worthwhile undertaking, success will require patience, persistence, practice, and hard work. Although this book will help you learn new self-fulfilling ways of thinking, feeling, and doing, it is not a complete therapy guide and will not substitute for a skilled therapist or counselor. Nevertheless, it does provide an opportunity to engage in some meaningful self-analysis and will help you overcome the anxiety and depression experienced by many adults on the autism spectrum. It will also serve as useful supplementary reading for many who have participated in counseling or therapy and as an adjunct resource for therapists. You are now ready to take an important step in learning new ways of thinking, feeling, and behaving.

# CHAPTER 2

# WHERE ARE YOU ON THE AUTISM SPECTRUM?

A major premise of this book is that autism is a spectrum condition and that autistic traits are distributed throughout the normal population. Yes, the "normal" population! The second premise is that we should view autism as a spectrum condition (not necessarily a disorder or disability). Third, autism should be viewed from a dimensional perspective, rather than an all-or-none category. Categories assume that everyone within that category is the same. Of course, this is not true.

## Disorder or condition?

According to the Diagnostic and Statistical Manual of Mental Disorders, Fifth Edition (DSM-5), autism spectrum disorder (ASD) is a neurodevelopmental disorder characterized by impairments in (a) social communication and (b) restricted and/or repetitive behaviors or interests that vary in severity of symptoms, age of onset, and association with other disorders (APA, 2013). Experts such as Simon Baron-Cohen (2008) contend that the term autism spectrum condition (ASC) is preferable to ASD, as this term concurrently recognizes both the problematic aspects of being on the autism spectrum and a profile of strengths (e.g., non-social skills). As with any human condition, an autism spectrum condition may or may not be disabling. While an individual with autism certainly thinks and perceives differently than the "typical" person, he or she may not be significantly impaired. For example, someone might demonstrate mild qualitative differences in social skills, yet not meet the clinical criteria for an autism spectrum condition. While a person's social skills might be below average relative to his or her age group, these differences may not result in what might be considered to be a "global" disability or impairment. Moreover, there are individuals without a clinical diagnosis who have significant difficulties, while others with a clinical diagnosis experience only mild problems. It is when these differences in social functioning lead to an impairment in adaptability (e.g., personal, social, occupational) and the need for direct support and clinical services, that we should describe the individual as having a disability. The term autism spectrum condition also communicates a value-free or neutral perception as opposed to the negative impression associated with disorder or disability. Last, the term "condition" acknowledges that individuals with autism spectrum conditions also possess positive traits, thus encouraging a strength-based perspective. The term autism spectrum condition (ASC) is used throughout this book.

## The autism spectrum

What is an autistic trait? A trait may be defined as a distinguishing feature of your personal nature. We might also think of a trait as a specific way of looking, thinking, and perceiving. Although individuals on the autism spectrum have different ways of learning, focusing attention, interacting, or reacting to sensations, we no longer accept the notion that the autism spectrum is clearly separated from what we often refer to as "normality" or "typicality." In fact, all of the features or traits that characterize autism spectrum conditions can be found in varying degrees in the normal or typical population (Baron-Cohen, 2008; Constantino and Todd, 2003).

What does it mean that autistic traits can be found in the normal or general population? A normal distribution is the bell curve that describes many traits (or characteristics) which vary across a group of individuals. Figure 2.1 shows the theoretical normal distribution curve. The normal curve has two tails. At the center of the curve is the mean or average for the population. The farther away you move from the average, the fewer the number of people with a specific trait. The vertical lines on either side of the mean are standard deviations (SD). A majority of the population falls within 2 SDs above and below the mean. Look between the vertical lines on the curve between -2 and +2. The percent of the scores are 13.5% + 34% + 34% + 13.5%, which totals 95%. A conservative definition of the average range or normality might include anyone falling within 2 SDs of the mean, with the remaining percentage representing the extreme ends of the curve. We can apply the normal curve to describe the distribution of many different traits in the general population (e.g., height, weight, blood pressure, intelligence, personality characteristics). For example, most people fall in the middle of the normal curve in terms of height, with a smaller number of people in each tail of the distribution (e.g., where fewer people are very tall or very short). You might also be familiar with the normal curve in terms of mental characteristics such as intelligence (IQ), where again, most people fall in the middle of the distribution and only a few at the extreme ends.

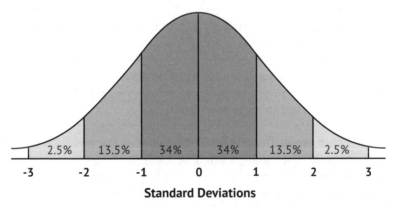

Figure 2.1: Normal distribution curve

## The autism spectrum quotient

Autistic traits are also normally distributed across the general population. In other words, we all have some autistic traits, just like we all have varying degrees of height, weight, and intelligence (Baron-Cohen, 2008). A self-report questionnaire called the Autism Spectrum Quotient (AQ) can be used to illustrate the distribution of autistic traits in the general population (Baron-Cohen *et al.*, 2001). Adults can complete the AQ to estimate how many autistic traits they might possess. Table 2.1 presents 10 items from the AQ. To illustrate, if you disagree with items 1, 3, 8, and 10, then you would receive 4 points on the AQ (e.g., four autistic traits). If you agree with the other items, then you would receive another 6 points (or a total of ten autistic traits). The complete AQ, scoring criteria, and interpretive guidelines are available in Appendix A (Baron-Cohen *et al.*, 2001; Baron-Cohen, 2004).

TABLE 2.1: ITEMS FROM THE ADULT AUTISM SPECTRUM QUOTIENT (AQ)

| |
|---|
| 1. I prefer to do things with others rather than on my own. |
| 2. I prefer to do the same things over and over again. |
| 3. If I try to imagine something, I find it very easy to create a picture in my head. |
| 4. I frequently get so strongly absorbed in one thing that I lose sight of other things. |
| 5. I often notice small sounds when others do not. |
| 6. I find it hard to make new friends. |
| 7. Other people frequently tell me that what I've said is impolite, even though I think it is polite. |
| 8. When I'm reading a story, I can easily imagine what the characters might look like. |

9. New situations make me nervous.

10. In a social group, I can easily keep track of several different people's conversations.

There are a total of 50 items in the full version of the AQ, so you will obtain a score somewhere between 0 and 50. The higher the score, the more autistic traits you have. Scores from 0 to 10 indicate very few autistic traits. Most typical individuals receive a score somewhere between 11 and 22, while scores from 23 to 31 indicate an above average number of autistic traits. A score of 32 or above indicates that one has a very high number of autistic traits. Most people with an autism spectrum condition score about 35 and fall at the extreme end (or high end) of this continuous distribution of autistic traits or behaviors. There is, however, considerable variation in the profiles of individuals on the spectrum. For example, there are individuals in the average range whose autistic traits adversely affect their adaptability. Conversely, there are some persons in the extreme range who do not require direct clinical support. The point here is that autism spectrum conditions occur on a continuum throughout the general population and vary in terms of severity and need for support. There are also gender differences on the AQ. Males tend to score higher on the AQ than females. For example, men have an average AQ score of 17 and women a score of 15. Although a small difference, this suggests that in the general population, males have more autistic traits than females. *A note of caution!* The AQ is NOT a diagnostic instrument and should not be use to classify or diagnose an individual. Only a trained and experienced mental health professional can diagnose an autism spectrum condition. Nevertheless, the AQ will give you an idea of where you might fall on the autism spectrum and can be helpful in your self-analysis. It is also important to remember that "typical" results are only averages, and many men and women differ in their scores.

## Comorbidity

The transition to adulthood can be challenging for many individuals on the autism spectrum as the social world becomes more complex and difficult to navigate. Social and communication problems frequently extend into adulthood, affecting interpersonal relationships and adaptability, which can lead to mental health difficulties such as anxiety and depression (Seltzer *et al.*, 2004). You may have heard the term *cormorbidity* used when discussing the autism spectrum. This term generally refers to a problem that co-exists or co-occurs with another problem so that both share a primary focus of attention. Comorbidity or co-existing problems appear to be the rule rather than the exception for individuals on the autism spectrum. Adults with autism exhibit greater levels of anxiety and depression, both of which can have an adverse effect on adjustment and quality of life (Anderson *et al.*, 2014; Attwood, 2006; Howlin, 2000; Joshi *et al.*, 2013; Mazzone, Ruta, and Reale, 2012). Although anxiety is not a defining characteristic of autism spectrum conditions, prevalence rates are significantly higher among individuals on the spectrum than in typical persons (Howlin, 2005; Ozsivadjian, Knott, and Magiati, 2012). There also appears to be a bidirectional (two-way) association between anxiety problems and autistic traits. For example, both a higher prevalence of anxiety problems has been found in persons on the spectrum, and a higher rate of autistic traits has been reported in individuals with anxiety problems. As you might expect, individuals on the spectrum display more social anxiety symptoms compared to typical individuals (Attwood, 2006; Cardaciotto and Herbert, 2004). A person might often feel socially awkward and overconcerned about what others think about them. Similarly, adults on the spectrum may find group situations and social communications worrisome because they are unsure of what is socially appropriate and have difficulty choosing a topic of conversation. Difficulties reading body language and facial expressions can also make a person on the spectrum feel anxious or nervous in social situations.

Depression is another common problem facing people with autism spectrum conditions (Atwood, 2006; Ghaziuddin, Ghaziuddin, and Greden, 2002; Howlin, 2000, 2005; Sterling *et al.*, 2008). Rates of depressive symptoms increase with age among individuals with autism spectrum conditions and are more prevalent than in typical men and women. Feelings of depression and sadness are often related to elevated stress levels, interpersonal difficulties, poor communication skills, problems with social connectedness, withdrawal, loneliness, and isolation (Mazurek, 2014). Contrary to popular assumptions, individuals on the autism spectrum do not always prefer solitude and seclusion. They may have a desire to develop social relationships, but face barriers in developing relationships due to their social skills difficulties. These social and interpersonal problems often persist into adulthood, increasing the risk for depression and contributing to functional impairment (Mazurek, 2014; Orsmond *et al.*, 2013). Problems associated with obsessive-compulsive behaviors, attention deficits, perfectionism, and anger management are frequently experienced by adults on the autism spectrum as well. We will discuss autism and emotions further in Chapter 4.

## Summary

In this chapter we discussed the categorical and dimensional views of autism spectrum conditions; disorder versus condition; and co-occurring conditions. You learned that autistic traits are continuously distributed in the general population and that we all have some autistic traits. The adult version of the Autism Spectrum Quotient (AQ) self-report questionnaire was discussed and is provided at the end of the book to give you an idea of where you might fall on the autism spectrum and to illustrate how autism spectrum conditions are not defined by a clear cut separation from what we refer to as normalcy or typicality. In the next chapter we focus on self-analysis and examine your cognitive style.

# CHAPTER 3

# SELF-ANALYSIS AND YOUR COGNITIVE STYLE

Now that you have an idea of where you might fall on the autism spectrum, it's time to engage in some introspection and analyze your strengths and weaknesses, or what I call your cognitive (learning and thinking) style. Another important aspect of understanding where you are on the spectrum is differentiating between self-analysis and self-diagnosis. Diagnosis can be defined as the process of identifying a medical condition or disease by its signs, symptoms, and from the results of various diagnostic tests and procedures. The implication of a diagnosis is that the individual is impaired, disordered, or disabled in some way. Although self-diagnosis may have appeal to some, it is an activity that provides little benefit (other than perhaps the comfort or distinction of belonging to a group or category). While seeking an autism diagnosis as an adult is difficult, assigning one to yourself can be especially self-defeating (and possibly incorrect) as well. Of course, we all have a story to tell and a diagnosis might lend credence to our musings. Although self-diagnosis may provide comfort or a rationalization for a person's behavior, it will do little to improve your mental health. If an individual is in need of clinical support or community assistance, they should seek the guidance of a credentialed and experienced professional. Only a trained and experienced professional, through careful review of the individual's medical and social history and interpretation of information gained from standardized measures, can diagnose and treat an autism spectrum condition.

Self-analysis, on the other hand, offers the opportunity to assess your strengths and weaknesses, and provides the foundation for developing strategies for coping with your emotional challenges. Self-analysis also implies an awareness of your own individuality and knowledge of your own character, feelings, motives and desires. In this chapter you will have an opportunity to examine your strengths and weaknesses and discover your cognitive style. We will discuss two specific theories that might account for your autistic traits, the weak central coherence and empathizing— systemizing (E–S) theories. Both theories conceptualize a normal continuum in cognitive style (there are no deficits here) and explain how your cognitive style might influence your daily interactions with the world around you. Self-analysis will also help you think more clearly and act more effectively when dealing with your practical day-to-day problems.

## Weak central coherence theory

Central coherence is the ability to understand the general meaning of information rather than focusing on each individual detail. It can be described as "getting the point," or gist, of things. It is the ability to pull information from different sources and experiences, both internal and external, in order to achieve a higher and more complex meaning (Frith, 1989). The ability to process information in wholes rather than parts allows us to give priority to understanding meaning, and to comprehend the context in which events occur. Central coherence is conceptualized as varying in the typical population, forming a range of cognitive styles that extend from strong coherence (e.g., tendency to miss details and concentrate on the general picture) to weak coherence or detail focus (e.g., good attention and memory for details). It is weak central coherence or a detail-focused processing cognitive style or bias that has been proposed to characterize autism spectrum conditions, in which the individual tends to favor part/ detail processing and does not see the "big picture" in everyday life (Happé, 2005). According to this theory, people on the autism spectrum tend to focus on small details and experience difficulty integrating information to arrive at a logical, global picture. In other words, they tend to get lost in the details. As a result, a person lacking in central coherence might be more vulnerable to misinterpreting situations and communications with others. Again, this processing bias should be considered a specific cognitive style, rather than a deficit.

The notion of weak coherence as a cognitive style or processing bias, rather than deficit, lends itself to a continuum approach, in which weak coherence is seen as one end of a normal distribution (think back to the normal curve) of cognitive style, and where people with autism spectrum conditions are positioned at the extreme end of this continuum. I'm sure that you are familiar with the expression, "Can't see the forest through the trees." It means that you tend to lose yourself in the details (trees) and forget the larger picture or vision (forest). Some people on the spectrum get so stuck on the details that the fine points become the overwhelming focus which can sometimes cause you to overlook the original idea. In other words, you become overly concerned with the details and just can't see the "bigger" picture. In fact, you may have all the details but have difficulty putting them together so that they form a logical whole. Another way of looking at this theory is that while most people see that "trees have leaves," you might see every kind of tree as having a completely different type of leaf. Individuals with weak central coherence might display the following autistic traits: (a) lack of reciprocity and poor social skills; (b) bigger picture planning difficulties; (c) excellent attention to detail; (d) superior spatial visualization and non-verbal conceptualization ability; (e) obsessions with systems and narrow interests; and (f) sensory hypersensitivity (Baron-Cohen, 2008; Happé, 2005). The opposite cognitive style or other end of the continuum, strong coherence, might be characterized as a tendency for global processing at the expense of attention and memory for detail. Thus, while the person with weak coherence may be poor at seeing the bigger picture, the person with strong coherence may not attend to the details of the picture.

## Empathizing–systemizing (E–S) theory

Like the weak central coherence theory, the empathizing-systemizing (E–S) theory describes a different cognitive style or way of thinking. The E–S theory attempts to explain many of the social-communication problems experienced by people on the autism spectrum by focusing on two factors or psychological dimensions, empathizing (E) and systemizing (S) (Baron-Cohen et al., 2005). Empathizing (E) is defined as the drive to identify emotions and thoughts in others and to respond to these appropriately. In contrast, Systemizing (S) is defined as the drive to analyze and construct systems, with the goal of identifying and understanding rules in order to predict systemic behavioral events (Baron-Cohen, 2004; Baron-Cohen et al., 2005). The E–S model assumes that we all have both systemizing and empathizing skills and that they are normally distributed across the population and independent of each other. Understanding these dimensions will help you identify some of the behaviors associated with being on the spectrum. For example, the E–S theory can help explain the following autistic traits (Baron-Cohen, 2008):

- preference for repetition and rigid behavior
- difficulty reading emotions
- difficulty coping in social groups
- difficulty seeing another person's perspective
- a tendency for black and white thinking
- difficulty reading emotions
- excellent understanding of a whole system

- superior attention to detail

- sensory hypersensitivity.

## Empathizing (E)

This dimension provides us with a way of making sense of other peoples' behavior and a natural way of responding to others. It is not simply about inferring what someone else is thinking or feeling, though this is an important part of empathizing. It consists of both affective (emotional) and cognitive (intellectual) components (Baron-Cohen, 2008; Baron-Cohen *et al.*, 2005). The affective component of empathizing involves feeling an appropriate emotion triggered by seeing/learning of another's emotion. When engaged in affective empathy, we vicariously experience the emotional states of others, understanding that our feelings are not ours, but rather those of the other person. Sympathy is also considered an affective component of empathy. It is the feeling or emotion triggered by seeing or learning of someone else's distress which moves you to want to take an action that will help ease their suffering. It is especially important to understand that a weakness in affective empathizing does not mean that an individual is callous, unfeeling, or indifferent.

The cognitive (or intellectual) component of empathy involves the understanding and/or predicting what someone else might think, feel, or do or what might be called Theory of Mind (ToM). ToM is the ability to identify cues that indicate the thoughts and feelings of others and "to put oneself into another person's shoes." It is also referred to as "mentalizing," "mindreading," and "perspective taking" (Baron-Cohen, 1995; Baron-Cohen, 2008; Baron-Cohen *et al.*, 2005; Wilkinson, 2011). The ability to reflect on one's own and other people's minds (beliefs, desires, intentions, imagination and emotions) allows us to interact effectively with others in the social world. ToM may also be thought of existing on a continuum with some individuals able to "mindread" relatively easily and intuitively, while others experience varying degrees of problems interpreting and predicting another person's behavior. Most (but not all) typical individuals are able to mindread relatively easily and intuitively. They can read another person's facial expression and body language, and tone of voice and recognize his or her thoughts and feelings, and the likely course of their behavior. In other words, they interpret, predict, and participate in social interaction automatically, and for the most part, intuitively. This attribution of mental states is a fundamental component of social interaction and communication. A weakness in ToM may result in an inability to appreciate other people's emotions and thoughts, and to make sense of or predict another's actions. This is sometimes called "mindblindness" (Baron-Cohen, 1995; Baron-Cohen, 2008; Wilkinson, 2011).

A weakness in ToM may leave a person puzzled by another's actions because their behavior may seem unpredictable. It is this lack of predictability that can make a person anxious and frustrated in social situations. So the next time you feel like saying (or say) to someone, "What am I, a mind reader?" you know that it's likely a case of not being able to identify the person's intentions behind their gestures and speech, and see the signals that might predict the person's actions or behavior. You can try your hardest to figure out someone's actions or what they are thinking, or likely to do next, or simply guess. Of course, your guess might be wrong! This will likely result in additional confusion, frustration, and anxiety, making social communication even more of a challenge. A weakness in perspective taking abilities might also be seen in a tendency to be somewhat rigid and uncompromising; an aversion to being interrupted by others; inflexible adherence to one's own perspective; and inattentiveness to others' interests. As a result, a person's behavior might be described by others as disrespectful, inconsiderate, and rude. It is also important to understand that cognitive empathy (ToM) can vary as a function of a person's emotional state. For example, feeling anxious, depressed, or angry might cloud your ability to see the other person's perspective, so that you are temporarily only able to see your own. Therefore, your ability to switch perspectives may be reduced by your current emotional state.

## The Empathy Quotient (EQ)   •

How can we determine our level of empathy? As with IQ, you have an EQ. The Empathy Quotient (EQ) is a self-report questionnaire that can be used to assess both the cognitive and affective aspects of empathy (Baron-Cohen and Wheelwright, 2004). You can use the EQ to get an idea of your empathizing traits. Ten items from the EQ are shown in Table 3.1. If you agree with items 1, 3 and 6 then you would receive three EQ points. If you disagree with the rest, you would have a total of 10 EQ points. The EQ has 60 items. The higher your score, the better your empathy. On average, most women score about 47 and most men about 42 on the EQ. Most people on the autism spectrum score about 20 out of a maximum score of 80. Once again, a score on the lower end of the continuum does not mean that an individual lacks kindness, feeling, and sensitivity. The full version of the EQ, including how to score and interpret the results, can be found in Appendix B (Baron-Cohen and Wheelwright, 2004; Baron-Cohen, 2004).

TABLE 3.1: ITEMS FROM THE ADULT EMPATHY QUOTIENT (EQ)

| |
|---|
| 1. I can easily tell if someone else wants to enter a conversation. |
| 2. I find it difficult to explain to others things that I understand easily, when they don't understand them the first time. |
| 3. I really enjoy caring for other people. |
| 4. I find it hard to know what to do in a social situation. |

*cont.*

| |
|---|
| 5. People often tell me that I went too far in driving my point home in a discussion. |
| 6. I am good at predicting how someone will feel. |
| 7. Friendships and relationships are just too difficult, so I tend not to bother with them. |
| 8. I often find it difficult to judge if something is rude or polite. |
| 9. In a conversation, I tend to focus on my own thoughts rather than on what my listener might be thinking. |
| 10. I find it hard to know what to do in a social situation. |

## Systemizing (S)

We now turn to the second psychological dimension of the E–S theory, systemizing. We learned that empathizing (E) is the drive to identify emotions and thoughts in others and to respond to these appropriately. The systematizing dimension is defined as the drive to analyze and construct systems, with the goal of identifying and understanding rules in order to predict systemic behavioral events (Baron-Cohen, 2004; Baron-Cohen *et al.*, 2005). We don't analyze systems in terms of emotions and mental states. Rather, we examine relationships between components and associations between events which then allow us to understand the underlying rules. When we systemize we try to identify the rules of the system in order to predict how that system will respond. This might be any kind of system. For example, systems can be (a) mechanical; (b) natural; (c) numerical; (d) spatial; (e) motoric; and (f) organizable. They may involve math, physics, chemistry, logic, music, and computer programming (Baron-Cohen, 2008). Systems also include libraries, economics, companies, taxonomies, board games, or sports. If you have strength in systemizing you will not only have a strong attention to detail, note regularities and rules, and understand how a particular system operates, but also be able to predict what the system will do next. Table 3.2 lists some examples of how individuals might show their strong systemizing in different ways.

TABLE 3.2: EXAMPLES OF SYSTEMIZING

| Sensory systemizing | *Insisting on the same foods each day* |
|---|---|
| Motoric systemizing | *Learning a specific golf or tennis technique* |
| Collectible systemizing | *Making lists and cataloguing items* |
| Numerical systemizing | *Solving math problems* |
| Mechanical systemizing | *Taking apart gadgets and reassembling them* |
| Natural systemizing | *Learning the Latin names of every plant and their optimal growing conditions* |
| Spatial systemizing | *Studying maps and routes* |
| Musical systemizing | *Analyzing the musical structure of a song* |
| Vocal/auditory/verbal systemizing | *Collecting words and word meanings* |
| Social systemizing | *Insisting on engaging in the same activity with others* |

*Source:* Adapted from Baron-Cohen (2008), pp.66–68.

## The Systemizing Quotient (SQ)

Another self-report questionnaire called the Systemizing Quotient (SQ) can help determine your preferences for systemizing (Baron-Cohen *et al.*, 2004). It includes items asking about your level of interest in a range of different systems that exist in the environment (including technical, abstract, and natural systems). Much like the AQ and EQ discussed earlier, you simply indicate whether you agree or disagree with each statement that describes you. Table 3.3 lists ten sample items from the SQ. For example, if you disagree with items 5, 7, and 9, you would receive three points. If you agree with the other items, you would earn another seven points, making a total of ten systemizing points. The higher your score, the stronger your drive or preference for systemizing. Unlike the EQ, people on the autism spectrum tend to score significantly higher on the SQ compared to the typical or normal population. Most adults on the spectrum score in the above average range (40–50) and three times as many more people with an autism spectrum condition score in the very high range (51–80). There are also gender differences. On average women score about 24 and men score about 30 out of a maximum score of 80 on the SQ. The complete version of the SQ is reproduced in Appendix C, together with information on scoring and interpretation (Baron-Cohen *et al.*, 2004; Baron-Cohen, 2004).

TABLE 3.3: ITEMS FROM THE ADULT SYSTEMIZING QUOTIENT (SQ)

| |
|---|
| 1. I prefer to read non-fiction than fiction. |
| 2. I am fascinated by how machines work. |
| 3. When I read something, I always notice whether it is grammatically correct. |
| 4. When I listen to a piece of music, I always notice the way it's structured. |
| 5. I find it difficult to read and understand maps. |
| 6. When I hear the weather forecast, I am not very interested in the meteorological patterns. |
| 7. I do not enjoy games that involve a high degree of strategy. |

| |
|---|
| 8. If I were buying a car, I would want to obtain specific information about its engine capacity. |
| 9. I do not read legal documents very carefully. |
| 10. When I am walking in the country, I am curious about how the various kinds of trees differ. |

## Your cognitive style

Once you have an idea of your EQ and SQ, it is possible to determine your particular cognitive type or style. It is the asymmetry or difference between dimensions (E–S), rather than E or S alone, that describes an individual's cognitive style, and differentiates typical males, females, and people with autism spectrum conditions. Figure 3.1 illustrates the main cognitive types or styles on axes of the empathizing (E) and systemizing (S) dimensions (numbers are standard deviations from the mean). Each cognitive style is determined by plotting the EQ score on the vertical axis and the SQ score on the horizontal axis. As you can see, the extreme types E and S lie at the outer borders. People with autism spectrum conditions tend to fall in the dark gray zone, that is, they have below average empathizing but above average or superior systemizing ability (Baron-Cohen, 2008).

Table 3.4 also shows the possible cognitive styles or types (Baron-Cohen, 2008). According to the E–S theory, individuals in whom empathizing is more developed than systemizing are referred to as Type E. Individuals in whom systemizing is more developed than empathizing are called Type S. Individuals in whom systemizing and empathizing are both equally developed are called Type B (balanced). Individuals whose empathy is above average, but who may be challenged when it comes to systemizing are called an Extreme Type E. In contrast, individuals whose systemizing is well developed but whose empathizing is challenged are considered an Extreme Type S. General population measures of empathy and systemizing suggest that most males have a Type S cognitive style or bias and most females have a Type E cognitive style or bias. Since the majority of individuals on the autism spectrum score significantly higher on the SQ, and significantly lower on the EQ, you are likely to have an Extreme Type S cognitive style (Baron-Cohen, 2008).

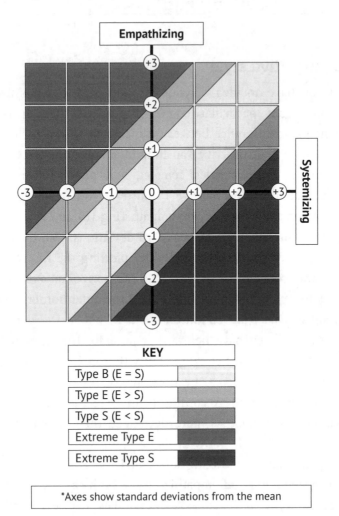

Figure 3.1: E–S scores and cognitive styles
*Source: Baron-Cohen (2008), p.73. Reproduced with permission.*

TABLE 3.4: POSSIBLE COGNITIVE STYLES

| Cognitive style | Description |
|---|---|
| 1. Balanced (B) | Empathy is the same as systemizing (E=S) |
| 2. Empathizing bias (E) | Stronger empathy than systemizing (E>S) |
| 3. Systemizing bias (S) | Systemizing stronger than empathy (S>E) |
| 4. Extreme empathizing bias | Empathy is above average but challenged with systemizing (E>>S) |
| 5. Extreme systemizing bias | Systemizing is above average but challenged with empathy (S>>E) |

## Cognitive style and behavior

How does your cognitive style help explain your autistic traits (behavior) and emotional response to people and situations? An individual's cognitive style can have notable advantages (as well as disadvantages) for day-to-day information processing. For example, an excellent "eye for detail," memory for facts, and knowledge of a specific topic can be a strength in many areas of life. While the average or typical individual might have difficulty attending to the details, you are unlikely to overlook differences that might be very important. On the other hand, you may take longer to make use of the larger context in a world that prefers a global processing style. Although looking out for the small details in life is generally a good practice, missing the big picture can present some problems. You may focus on a rule or detail in one situation but have difficulty making connections and applying it to another situation because you may not see a common thread. Being so detail-oriented, you may also have difficultly choosing or prioritizing and organizing material and experiences. Thus, small changes in the environment might be quite distressing. Difficulties in integrating information into a coherent whole and a tendency to process information piece by piece often leads people on the autism spectrum to experience the world in a disjointed way, resulting in a poor understanding of social meaning. This weakness in ability to conceptualize whole pieces of information might result in a preference for attending to details and a reliance on rote memory in order to make sense of the constantly changing world. In fact, a lack of central coherence or gestalt processing can easily cause a person to miss the importance of the subtle cues that create meaning in a social context, including difficulty intuitively understanding the main idea or gist of a conversation and thus, the relevance.

In terms of the E–S dimensions, below average empathy might explain a lack of reciprocity and poor social skills. Likewise, above average systemizing might explain much of your non-social behaviors such as narrow or restricted interests and preference for routines (Baron-Cohen, 2004). If you are a strong systemizer, you likely have a superior memory for details and facts and are strongly drawn to structured, factual, and rule-based information. Unlike the average person who might not notice important details, you seldom miss key differences in objects and systems. In fact, a high level of systemizing ability can lead to considerable achievement in mathematics, mechanical knowledge and other factual, scientific, technical, or rule-based subjects and professions. Unfortunately, systemizing is not generally helpful for predicting the moment-by-moment changes in another person's behavior. To effectively predict human behavior, empathizing is required. So, although you may be a strong systemizer, a weakness in empathizing may result in difficulty attributing mental states to others, and responding appropriately to the another person's emotional state. In fact, someone who relies on systemizing to predict people's behavior would most likely conclude that people are unpredictable and not clearly rule-governed. Although a talented systemizer, your ToM problems or "mindblindness" may leave you puzzled by an individual's actions and anxious because the other person's behavior seems unpredictable. A systemizing bias might also lead to problems generalizing to other systems and situations. Likewise, you might have a strong resistance to change and/or have a need for sameness. You might lack flexibility and have difficulty stepping outside the rules (becoming rule bound) and dealing with the unpredictability of everyday life (Grandin and Barron, 2005). Strength in systemizing might also explain your preference for repetition in games, need for routine, and difficulty in turn taking. Likewise, this may account for problems with emotion regulation and distress when faced with an abrupt change in routine or a different point of view or perspective (Baron-Cohen, 2004).

It is important to remember that these cognitive styles or types represent only biases (Baron-Cohen *et al.*, 2005; Happé, 2005). The person with strong coherence can, by effort, compensate and turn their attention to details such as remembering unconnected facts for a test, just as the individual with weak coherence can learn to extract the general idea of a lengthy verbal presentation. In fact, weak coherence and extreme Type S cognitive styles can be found in well-adapted, healthy and capable adults, most notably in professions where attention to detail may be important. (e.g., engineering, computer science, mathematics). There is a good chance that over time you will achieve a good understanding of the whole system and process more globally for meaning when explicitly required to do so. You should view your detail-focused processing and systemizing cognitive style as being highly purposeful because it helps you understand the details and rules of a complex situation or system (Baron-Cohen, 2008).

A final comment regarding the weak central coherence and E–S theories of autism. In psychology, theories are used to provide a model for understanding human thoughts, emotions and behaviors. By definition, a theory is an idea or set of ideas that is intended to explain facts or events, but is not known or proven to be true. It is important to remember that weak central coherence and E–S are theories and that they are among several that seek to explain the behavior and psychological profile of individuals with autism spectrum conditions. Likewise, they may not explain all of the characteristics or features associated with being on the autism spectrum or account for the whole range of autistic traits. As with the AQ in the previous chapter, the EQ and SQ are not diagnostic nor are they intended for self-diagnosis. No single score on any of these tests or questionnaires indicates that an individual has an autism spectrum condition. A diagnosis is the result of an extensive assessment, not the result of a test score, and is typically relevant for individuals who are seeking assistance and are in need of direct clinical support. As noted earlier, only a credentialed and experienced professional should make a diagnosis of an autism spectrum condition.

## Summary

In this chapter, you were introduced to the weak central coherence and E–S theories and how they account for many of your autistic traits. You also had an opportunity to determine your particular cognitive style. Although this information will help you to understand how your autistic traits might influence your everyday life and relationships, it will not automatically tell you what causes your emotional upsets or how to overcome your anxiety and depression. In other words, self-analysis and insight is not enough. In the next chapter, we focus on the basic tenet of CBT, the ABCs of emotions. Here you will learn the connection between your thoughts and feelings, and how you create your own appropriate and inappropriate feelings.

# CHAPTER 4

# THE ABCs OF EMOTIONS

This chapter introduces you to the ABC theory of emotions (feelings). There are three major features of human functioning: thoughts or cognition, feelings, and behavior. The first and most fundamental principle of CBT is that cognition is the most important cause of human emotion (Beck, 1995; DeRubeis *et al.*, 2010; Dryden *et al.*, 2010). Events and other people do not make us feel good or feel bad; we do it to ourselves, cognitively or in our heads (Ellis, 1988; Ellis and Harper, 1975). In other words, if we think about problems in an anxious, depressed, or angry manner, we will feel anxious, depressed, and angry. If people change the way in which they think about an event or situation, they will most likely feel differently about it and change the way in which they respond to it (Walen, DiGiuseppe, and Wessler, 1980). Past or present events contribute to, but do not directly cause our emotions. Rather, it is our perceptions, inferences, beliefs, and ideas about these events that are the most direct and influential sources of our emotional responses (Dryden *et al.*, 2010; Ellis and Harper, 1975; Walen *et al.*, 1980). It is the way we think about things that upsets us, not the events themselves. More simply stated, *we feel the way we think.*

## ABC framework

The ABC framework is the cornerstone of CBT (Dryden *et al.*, 2010; Dryden and DiGiuseppe, 1990; Ellis and Dryden, 1987, 2007).

Figure 4.1 displays the ABC model of emotions. **A** stands for an activating event or situation. This situation need not always be an external event in one's environment. In fact, memories, thoughts, emotions, and physiological sensations can form an internal activating event. **B** represents your belief system (cognitions, thoughts, views, opinions, meanings, attitudes, ideas, perceptions, and expectations). The **C** in the **ABC** framework stands for the emotional and behavioral consequences about **A**. They are your feelings or emotions (e.g. anxiety, depression, anger). Most of us think that **A** causes **C**. Rather, it is **B**, the belief about **A**, which largely causes **C**, or the emotional consequence.

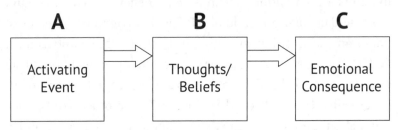

Figure 4.1: ABC model of emotions

Whenever your goals are blocked by an unfortunate activating event (your A) and whenever you feel upset at the consequences (your C), you tend to incorrectly blame C on A. You might think, because I was socially rejected at A and because I feel depressed at C, A causes C. In other words, you wrongly conclude that rejection causes you to feel depressed. While A might contribute to C, it never really causes the negative emotional consequence. It is your B or belief or thought about A that causes you to feel anxious, depressed, or angry. When you say "That makes me feel anxious or depressed," or "You made me angry," it is more appropriate to say "I made myself nervous or depressed about that," and "I angered myself about your behavior." Try a practice exercise to identify the ABCs of common situations which might produce some emotional distress for you. Think of an event or occasion where you were emotionally upset. Next, how did you feel (anxious, depressed, angry)? What were you telling yourself about the event or situation? What thoughts were you thinking when you felt this upsetting emotion? What did you do? What was your behavior? Use the ABC Worksheet in Appendix D to practice identifying the ABCs of emotions in your daily life.

When a negative event (A) happens, we can interpret it positively or negatively (B). How you interpret or perceive it affects how you feel, think, and behave (C). Here is an example (Vivyan, 2013). If someone you know passes you on the street without acknowledging you, you can interpret it several ways. You might think they ignored you because they don't like you (which may cause you to feel depressed), you might hope they don't stop to talk to you because you won't know what to say and they'll think you're socially inept (making you feel anxious), or you may think that they are deliberately ignoring you (leading to anger). A healthier, more balanced thought might be that they were distracted by something else and just didn't notice you. Another example may be that someone who feels depressed might wake up in the morning and think: "This is going to be another terrible day. Nobody likes me. I'll only make another mistake at work," and "Everything is hopeless!" It is very likely that these negative thoughts will only increase the person's feelings of despair and result in further social isolation. Because particular types of thoughts tend to lead to particular emotions, this can lead to a sequence of events in which you continue to think and act the same way over and over again. In other words, you make yourself anxious about your anxiety, depressed about your depression, and angry about your anger. A discussion of these emotions will help you to understand the connection between your thoughts and feelings and how the vicious cycles of anxiety, depression, and anger maintain your emotional upsets.

## Anxiety

We all feel anxious sometimes. In fact, a certain amount of anxiety helps us to be more alert and focused. For example, feeling anxious just before an important exam at school or presentation at work can have a positive effect by motivating and helping to focus our thoughts on the task before us. On the other hand, intense anxiety or constantly being anxious is unhealthy and detrimental to our personal lives and relationships. The cognitive distortions and errors in thinking that occur in anxiety often include overestimating or exaggerating the actual threat or danger, and underestimating or minimizing our ability to cope. You might think to yourself "I'm in danger right now," "The worst possible scenario is going to happen," "I'm afraid of what's going to happen," or "I won't be able to cope with this situation." Anxiety might also be related to an overconcern for what someone might think about you, excessive worry as to whether you will be accepted by others, or an intense fear of making a mistake in public. Although an important part of almost every aspect of life, decision-making can be especially difficult for adults on the spectrum. Decisions and judgments that need to be made quickly, involve a change of routine, or talking to others can be exhausting, overwhelming, and anxiety-provoking (Luke *et al.*, 2012). Not surprisingly, adults on the autism spectrum are likely to avoid the decision-making process. Changes and disruptions to routines, sensory sensitivities, specific fears, confusion and worry about social expectations, and difficulties in perspective-taking (ToM) can all serve as specific triggers for anxiety (Ozsivadjian *et al.*, 2012). Unusual sensory responses such as oversensitivity to daily aspects of the environment are relatively common in autism spectrum conditions and have been linked to high rates of anxiety. For example, the more autistic traits you endorse on the Autism Spectrum Quotient (AQ), the more likely you are to experience an increase in both sensory sensitivity problems and anxiety symptoms (Horder *et al.*, 2014; Tavassoli *et al.*, 2014). Everyday experiences and situations that may be tolerable for most typical individuals might be stressful, fear-provoking, disturbing, or irritating for someone on the autism spectrum. As a result, you may avoid many important life activities or be in a constant state of anxiety and unable to function at an optimal level because of your fears, worry, and sensory processing issues. Figure 4.2 shows the vicious cycle of anxiety.

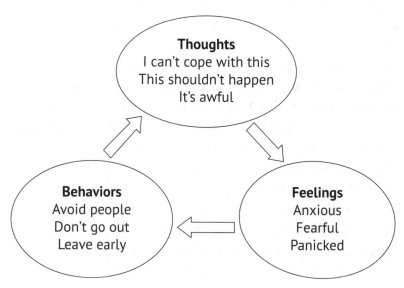

Figure 4.2: Cycle of anxiety

## Depression

Sadness or downswings in mood are normal reactions to life's hassles, setbacks, and disappointments. The typical ups and downs of life mean that we all feel sad or have the "blues" at times. Although everyone occasionally feels depressed, intense and persistent feelings of hopelessness, despondency, and guilt interfere with daily functioning and cause distress for both the person and those around him or her. As noted earlier, depression is one of the most common co-occurring (comorbid) conditions observed in individuals on the autism spectrum, with rates significantly higher than would be expected in the general population. Of course, feelings of depression are an understandable reaction to employment difficulties, relationship issues, loneliness, and social rejection when trying to understand and adapt to the social world. The trigger stimulus for depression is often the loss of someone or something very important, a disappointment, a perceived harm to self-esteem, feelings of loneliness, social rejection, and isolation. Feelings of loneliness and social isolation have been shown to increase negative emotional experiences and the risk of depression, which can contribute to reduced life satisfaction and psychological well-being (Mazurek 2014; Orsmond *et al.*, 2013). Adults on the autism spectrum often have difficulty interacting appropriately with others, establishing and maintaining friendships, and being able to predict what will happen in many typical situations. This lack of perspective taking and problems with social connectedness and reciprocity may leave you feeling isolated, rejected, and hopeless. Depression may also be accompanied by feelings of guilt, shame, anger, and anxiety. As a result, you may feel anxious, restless, and agitated much of the time and withdraw more than usual from others.

People who are depressed tend to think very negatively about themselves, the future, and the world around them. They may have strong feelings of worthlessness and severely criticize themselves for perceived faults and mistakes, telling themselves that everything is hopeless and that nothing can change. The world may be viewed as a terrible place where everything goes wrong. Negative thoughts and attributions include: "I'm useless, worthless," "It's entirely my fault," and "There's no hope, nothing will change." Unfortunately, you might dwell on these thoughts repeatedly, brood over things, think regretful things about the past, and question what you should or shouldn't have done. Physical symptoms are also associated with depression. These include fatigue, difficulty concentrating, changes in eating and sleeping patterns, and a loss of interest in previously enjoyed activities. The combination of negative thoughts and physical symptoms can result in a tendency to withdraw more and more from life activities and avoid family and friends. While most depressed people are able to continue their daily activities, including going to work and school, they do not function at an optimal level. The person may recognize the self-defeating nature of his or her behavior but is unable to act differently, and so continues with it. As a result, they may now "feel bad about feeling bad" and about its impact on their life and others. Figure 4.3 illustrates this vicious cycle of depression.

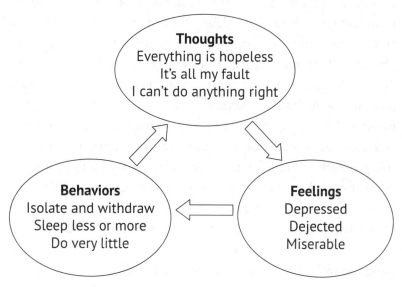

Figure 4.3: Cycle of depression

## Anger

Anger is one of the most common human emotions. However, some people tend to become angry more easily than others and have problems managing their anger. In fact, many adults on the autism spectrum experience problems with anger management. Anger has consequences and can cause problems in our personal and social lives. After an angry outburst, we might think critically of ourselves and our behavior, leading us to feel guilty and embarrassed. This might lower our mood and result in avoiding or withdrawing from others, and not wanting to engage in social activities. Because of your cognitive style and poor social information processing, you might often feel that you have been unfairly treated or disrespected, or that others have broken or fallen short of your rules, standards or expectations. Inflexible adherence to routines and a lack of problem-solving can trigger a maladaptive emotional response when faced with an unexpected change or transition. Sensory reactivity problems can also be distressing and lead to feelings of frustration, which can have an adverse impact on social functioning and disrupt daily living activities (Mazurek, Kanne, and Wodka, 2013; Tavassoli et al., 2014). Because adults on the spectrum may hear or feel things more intensely than the average person, you may have a negative emotional response to some sensory stimuli and feel frustrated and angered by common sounds in the environment. Likewise, being prevented from engaging in a preferred activity or interest or an abrupt change in routine might also produce irritability and anger. Thoughts may include, "I'm being treated unfairly," "I'm being disrespected," "They're breaking the rules," "It's not fair," or "I won't tolerate it." There may be a tendency to respond to these thoughts, by acting, or feeling an urge to act, in threatening or aggressive ways. Behaviors might include: staring and angry facial expressions; aggressive body posture; arguing or shouting; running or storming off; refusing to speak; and sulking. The vicious cycle of anger is illustrated in Figure 4.4.

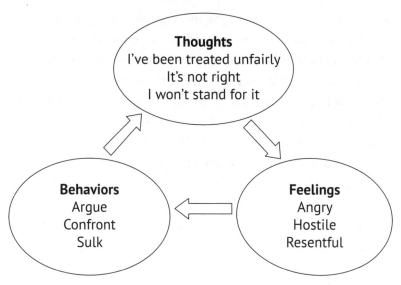

Figure 4.4: Cycle of anger

## Automatic thoughts

Don't confuse your emotions with your thoughts. Remember, emotions are mostly caused by our cognitions, thoughts, beliefs, ideas, and perceptions. These thoughts or beliefs tend to occur randomly and automatically (Beck, 1995). They are triggered whenever something happens to us or when we notice something in our surroundings. Although we may not realize it, our thoughts continually help us interpret and make sense of the world around us. They can be related to words, images, memories, physical sensations, imagined sounds, or simply based on what we often call intuition (Vivyan, 2013). Our thoughts tend to be quite specific to us and are uniquely ours. Because of our previous experiences, background, knowledge, culture, and religious beliefs and values, we may interpret and evaluate situations or events differently than someone else. For example, we might think that something is enjoyable or horrible, good or bad, dangerous or safe while another person may not share the same perception of the event. As we learned in the previous chapter, it is the interpretations and meanings we give the events and situations in our lives that drive our emotions and feelings (DeRubeis *et al.*, 2010; Dryden *et al.*, 2010). Likewise, different emotions are often associated with particular types of thoughts. For example, thinking that you are not very good at talking with people may make you feel anxious or worried when out in social situations; thinking that no one likes you may make you feel depressed; and thinking that you always make mistakes and never get things right may make you angry with yourself. Table 4.1 illustrates some common thoughts and corresponding emotions. Use the Thought–Feeling Worksheet in Appendix E to practice identifying your thoughts and corresponding feelings.

TABLE 4.1: EXAMPLES OF THOUGHTS AND FEELINGS

| THOUGHT: I think that... | FEELING: As a result, I feel... |
|---|---|
| Nobody likes me... | ...depressed, dejected, lonely. |
| He embarrassed me on purpose... | ...angry, hostile, vengeful. |
| I can't cope with this situation... | ...anxious, helpless, fearful. |
| I've solved problems like this before... | ...hopeful, confident, optimistic. |
| This job doesn't have to be perfect... | ...relieved, comforted, reassured. |
| I've done the best that I can with this project... | ...pleased, satisfied, positive. |

## Unhelpful thinking habits

We all have some negative or dysfunctional automatic thoughts. They might also be described as thinking errors, cognitive distortions, or unhelpful thinking habits (Beck, 1995; DeRubeis *et al.*, 2010). Because our thoughts are habitual and persistent, they repeat themselves, and the more they recur, the more they seem credible. As a result, we tend to routinely believe our thoughts without debating or questioning their validity. Unfortunately, negative automatic thoughts are not necessarily true or helpful. They can lead to self-doubt, depression, anxiety, anger, guilt, irritability, and low mood. The difference between whether you accept and believe them or challenge and dispute them will have an influence on your emotional well-being. Table 4.2 shows some of our most common cognitive distortions or unhelpful thinking habits (Beck, 1995; DeRubeis *et al.*, 2010; Dryden *et al.*, 2010; Vivyan, 2013).

TABLE 4.2: UNHELPFUL THINKING HABITS

| | |
|---|---|
| *Demand thinking*: Operating by rigid rules and not allowing flexibility. Involves should, must, or ought statements. You tell yourself that you, others, and the world should, must or ought to be the way you decide them to be. Otherwise, it is awful, terrible, and unfair and you can't bear it, and/or won't stand for it. | *Mind Reading*: Making assumptions about other people's thoughts, feelings, and behavior without checking the evidence. Assuming that you know what others are thinking about you (e.g., they don't like me). |

*cont.*

| | |
|---|---|
| *All-or-nothing thinking*: Things are viewed in black and white categories or extremes. Believing that something or someone can only be good or bad, right or wrong with no middle ground. Perfectionism is related to this type of thinking. Unless a task is performed perfectly, you see yourself as a failure or if it isn't going to be perfect, there's no reason to try. | *Emotional reasoning*: Mistaking feelings for facts. Negative things you feel about yourself are considered to be true because they feel true. You assume that because you feel bad, the situation must be bad or you feel like a failure, therefore you are a failure. |
| *Overgeneralizing*: Coming to an overall negative conclusion based on a single negative event or piece of evidence. If something bad happens, you expect it to happen again. Includes words such as "always" or "never." You weren't selected for a promotion and think that you will "never" advance your career. | *Labeling*: Assigning labels to yourself and others. Because you made a mistake, you label yourself as a failure or hopeless. Labeling can also be applied to another person, which unfairly generalizes about that individual in a negative way. |
| *Discounting the positive*: You minimize any positive experiences by telling yourself that they don't count. If congratulated on a good job you may insist that anyone could have done it or that it should it have been done much better. Or, you may think people don't like you and discount those who show that they do. | *Personalizing and blame*: Taking responsibility for events or situations that are not your fault or entirely under your control. Conversely, you blame other people for your problems. You might think that your life is terrible because others don't support you. Blame prevents you from taking responsibility for your life. |

| | |
|---|---|
| *Mental filtering:* Concentrating on the negative while ignoring the positive. Or, not seeing things as they really are and interpreting events/situations in a negative irrational/distorted way. Only noticing your failures and not your successes. | *Catastrophic thinking or awfulizing:* You make out situations to be much worse than they actually are and imagine the absolute worst case scenario. You predict that you will not do a good job with a presentation and expect to make a total fool of yourself. It will be awful and unbearable. |

Although some unhelpful thinking habits may be more common than others, they mostly occur before and during a distressful event or situation. For example, use your feelings as a cue, and whenever you are feeling intensely upset, try and notice exactly how you are feeling (e.g., anxious, depressed, angry). Now ask yourself, "What was I thinking just then?" "Is this one of my unhelpful thinking habits?" The questions in Table 4.3 will help you to practice noticing these thoughts and feelings (Cully and Teten, 2008). The more you practice, the more you will be able to identify them and make helpful and effective changes. Use the Unhelpful Thinking Habits Record Form in Appendix F each day to keep a daily record of your dysfunctional and negative thought(s) and find more balanced alternatives. For example, a more balanced thought for your demand thinking might be "Am I putting undue pressure on myself by insisting that I 'must' do well? What would be a more realistic expectation?" If you find yourself engaging in all-or-nothing thinking, you might say to yourself, "Things aren't always black and white. There are shades of gray. Things don't have to be perfect." A more realistic thought for emotional reasoning might be "Just because it feels bad, doesn't mean it is bad. I'm just reacting to my thoughts." Or, if you are mind reading, ask yourself, "Am I assuming I know what the other person is thinking? Where's the evidence?"

Identifying and responding to your unhelpful thinking habits in a more healthy way can help break the vicious cycles of anxiety, depression, and anger and allow you to see the situation more clearly, and begin a positive shift in your emotional life. We will discuss ways of disputing and debating unrealistic and irrational thoughts in Chapter 5.

TABLE 4.3: HELPFUL QUESTIONS

| Event/situational questions | Thought questions | Feeling questions |
|---|---|---|
| Where did this event occur? What happened? What was I doing at the time? Who else was there? Who was I talking to? | What was going through my mind before I started to feel that way? What other thoughts did I have at that time? Which thought upset me most? What images did I have with these thoughts? What was I afraid might happen? What could have happened if this were true? What other ways could I think about this? | What emotion was I feeling before this event happened? How did I feel while it was happening? How would I rate the intensity of my feeling at the time (1–10)? What was my mood after this happened? |

## Learning to see the bigger picture

When something is distressing to us, we are frequently so close and involved with the situation that it is difficult to take a step back from what is happening and see a larger perspective. Think back to our discussion of weak central coherence. Much like weak central coherence, you may be stuck on the details and not see the bigger picture. However, we can try changing our view and like a camera lens, adjust the zoom setting to make it appear larger or smaller. As we zoom out, the camera focuses on a bigger picture and less on the details. Realistic and balanced thinking will help you to step back and be more aware of the bigger picture, which in turn, will help you respond in more helpful and effective ways. So, when confronted with a stressful event or situation, stop and ask yourself:

- What would be the best thing for me to do for this situation?

- What am I reacting to? What does this situation mean to me?

- What would this look like to others involved in the situation?

- What would this look like to someone else outside of the situation and not emotionally involved?

(adapted from Vivyan, 2013, p.37)

You should also realize that because of your detail-focused cognitive style, it may take a bit longer for you to see and make use of the larger context. When confronted with a stressful situation, exercise patience and restraint when responding and work hard to see the bigger picture. Stop and step back! Don't react immediately! Try to see the situation as an outside observer. You will find that seeing different perspectives will help reduce distressing emotions, make you feel more confident, and improve your social communication and relationships. If you persist in identifying your unhelpful thinking habits and biased perspectives, you will see things in a more balanced and realistic way. Likewise, you will discover that situations and people can be different from how we usually interpret things, which can lead to changes in how you view the world and bring about positive change.

## Summary

In this chapter, you learned the ABCs of emotions (feelings) and that it is our belief about an event or situation that causes our upsetness. In other words, we mostly feel the way we think. We discussed automatic thoughts and unhelpful thinking habits, and the vicious cycles of anxiety, depression, and anger. You also learned the importance of seeing the larger view and understanding different perspectives. Because our thoughts have a major impact on the way we feel, changing our unhelpful thoughts to more balanced and realistic ones is the key to overcoming anxiety and depression. A critical step in CBT is to learn how to identify and dispute the distorted thoughts and beliefs that cause your emotional upsets and self-defeating behaviors. Disputing is the **D** of the ABC model. The next chapter outlines the major categories of irrational beliefs (iBs). You will learn how to think scientifically, utilize disputing as an intervention to challenge these distorted and irrational beliefs, and substitute them with rational and appropriate feelings and behaviors. Realize that you are quite capable of thinking your way out of your anxiety and depression. Remember, when you change your thinking, you change your feelings!

# CHAPTER 5

# RATIONALITY AND SCIENTIFIC THINKING

As humans we have self-awareness. We can observe and evaluate our own goals, desires, and purposes. We can examine, analyze, and change them. In the preceding chapter, we discussed the ABC framework of CBT in which you learned how activating events (A) in your life do not directly cause your emotional consequences (C). Rather, it is your belief system (B) that largely upsets you. You also learned that we all engage in some dysfunctional thoughts and unhelpful thinking habits. Having learned that our thoughts are automatic, habitual, and not necessarily true, the next step involves challenging and changing your unhealthy and distorted beliefs. In this chapter, you will learn to use your good attention to detail and reliance on facts to think like a scientist and dispute the irrational and distorted beliefs that lead to your feelings of anxiety and depression. The goal is to help you internalize a broad range of rational and realistic beliefs, reconceptualize your ideas about your autistic traits, and become better able to more effectively deal with events and situations that cause you distress. You will also learn the importance of self-acceptance and that you are in control of your own emotional destiny.

## Rationality

What is rationality? Rational means reasonable, logical, efficient, and non-self-defeating. It also means that your thoughts are derived from objective fact rather than subjective opinion. Rational thinking involves looking at yourself, others, and the world in a balanced and reasonable way, without being overly negative or positive. Our belief system consists of two main types of beliefs or views of world, irrational beliefs (iBs) and rational beliefs (rBs) (Ellis and Harper, 1975; Ellis, 1988). Irrational beliefs are thoughts that help you feel inappropriately and behave ineffectively. They are characterized by strong demands such as "must," "have to," "should," "need," and all-or-nothing thinking. An irrational belief is not supported by the evidence and usually represents an overgeneralization. In contrast, rational beliefs are thoughts that help you feel appropriately and behave effectively. They are flexible and involve a preference rather than a rigid and absolute demand. A rational belief is supported by the evidence, moderates emotion, and helps attain your goals. Irrational beliefs are associated with inappropriate anxiety, depression, and anger while rational thoughts leave you feeling appropriately concerned, sad, and annoyed (Dryden *et al.*, 2010; Ellis, 1988). Table 5.1 illustrates the type of belief and appropriateness of emotional response (Dryden and DiGiuseppe, 1990).

TABLE 5.1: INAPPROPRIATE AND APPROPRIATE NEGATIVE EMOTIONS

| Inference perception | Type of belief | Emotion | Appropriateness of emotion |
|---|---|---|---|
| Threat or danger | Irrational | Anxiety | Inappropriate |
| | Rational | Concern | Appropriate |
| Loss or failure | Irrational | Depression | Inappropriate |
| | Rational | Sadness | Appropriate |
| Breaking of rule (self or other) | Irrational | Damning anger | Inappropriate |
| | Rational | Annoyance | Appropriate |

Although we all engage in unhelpful thinking habits and think irrationally from time to time, we can work at eliminating this tendency. Of course, it's unlikely that one can completely do away with the inclination to think irrationally, but you can reduce the frequency, the duration, and the intensity of these beliefs by continually revisiting the ABCs of emotions discussed in the previous chapter. Remember, we don't get upset by events or situations, but mainly upset ourselves by holding inflexible thoughts and beliefs about them. Likewise, it doesn't really matter when and how we start upsetting ourselves, we continue to feel upset because we hang on to these beliefs. The only way to overcome your feelings of anxiety, depression and anger is to work hard at identifying, disputing, and changing your dysfunctional beliefs. This takes practice, practice, and more practice. Complete the exercise in Table 5.2 to practice identifying rational and irrational beliefs.

TABLE 5.2: IDENTIFY THE iB AND rB EXERCISE

| As an exercise, review the following statements and see how many you can correctly identify as rational or irrational. The answers are on the last page of this chapter. |
| --- |
| 1. I wish I had succeeded at X; it would have made life a lot easier. |
| 2. It's awful that things didn't work out the way I expected. |
| 3. I can't stand listening to that awful music. |
| 4. What a disappointment that I didn't get the job. |
| 5. That driver should get a ticket for not obeying the speed limit. |
| 6. I wish we lived closer to the store so I wouldn't have to drive as far. |

*cont.*

| |
|---|
| 7. I must do well on this exam. |
| 8. I prefer that my supervisor not change my work schedule. |
| 9. This assignment has to be perfect or else I'll fail. |
| 10. This exercise is annoying. |

It is important to understand that analyzing and reasoning when carried to the extreme can be ineffective. For example, if every time you started your car or brewed a cup of coffee, you had to stop and reason whether this action was the right thing to do or the best way to do it, your reasoning would be more of a hindrance rather than a help. Extreme or obsessive-compulsive reasoning is really irrational and self-defeating (Ellis and Harper, 1975). Similarly, although CBT advocates a reasoned approach, it does not support rationalizing or intellectualizing as a way to overcome your emotional upsets. Rational thinking and rationalizing are not the same thing. Rationalizing means to offer seemingly rational and plausible explanations for one's actions, beliefs, desires, and behaviors. Rationalizing (or in essence excusing) your behavior is really the opposite of thinking rationally about it. Likewise, to intellectualize means to obsessively think about your emotional upsets in such a detailed and irrational way so as to avoid rather than deal with them (Ellis and Harper, 1975). Therefore, it is especially important to tackle your perfectionism and avoid getting "stuck" on the details at the expense of moving forward and overcoming your anxiety and depression.

## List of ten irrational beliefs

The thoughts that create our emotional upsets have been carefully studied and evaluated. Below are the ten major categories of irrational beliefs (iBs) that create most of our psychological distress and emotional upsets (Ellis and Harper, 1975;

Hauck, 1980; Walen *et al.*, 1980). Nearly all of our unrealistic beliefs and ideas, distorted automatic thoughts, and unhelpful thinking habits can be subsumed under these broad groupings. Following each irrational belief, you will find a description of its rational equivalent. Read each one carefully and note how these irrational beliefs create our feelings of anxiety, depression, and anger by representing demands, shoulds, musts, and needs. In fact, the beliefs that upset us might be considered variations of three core irrational beliefs. Each one contains an absolute must or demand, either about (1) ourselves, (2) other people, or (3) the world in general (Dryden *et al.*, 2010). Review each corresponding rational alternative belief and note how a healthier alternative thought reflects preferences and desires rather than rigid commands and demands.

---

**Irrational Belief # 1:** You must—yes, must—have sincere love and approval almost all the time from all the people you find significant.

---

*Rational Alternative Beliefs:* (a) I would like to be approved by every significant person, but I do not need such approval; (b) If I am not approved by someone I want to like me, I can try to determine what it is that person does not like about my behavior and decide whether I want to change it; (c) If I decide that this rejection is not based on any inappropriate behavior on my part, I can find others I can enjoy being with; (d) I might not like negative criticism or disapproval from others, but I can learn to tolerate it.

**Irrational Belief # 2:** You must prove yourself thoroughly competent, adequate, and achieving, at all times, or you must at least have real competence or talent in some important area.

*Rational Alternative Beliefs:* (a) I would like to be perfect or the best at this task, but I do not need to be; (b) I'm still successful when I do things imperfectly; (c) What I do doesn't have to be perfect to be good; (d) I may be happier if I am successful, but success does not determine my worth as a person, unless I let it; (e) I will be happier if I maintain a realistic rather than a perfect level of aspiration; (f) If I am not successful, I will likely be unhappy but not depressed and miserable; (g) It is best to accept oneself as an imperfect human being with weaknesses and limitations.

**Irrational Belief # 3:** You have to view life as awful, terrible, horrible, or catastrophic when you get seriously frustrated, treated unfairly, or rejected.

*Rational Alternative Beliefs:* (a) I don't like this situation. Now let me see what I can do to change it. If I can't change it, it will remain unpleasant but not awful or terrible; (b) Although I may find it unpleasant or unfortunate when I do not get what I want out of life, it is not horrible or catastrophic; (c) If I face serious frustration and there is no way to change or control it, then I can realistically accept it. I can then begin to make plans for making my life as pleasing and enjoyable as I can; (d) It is unfortunate that I have experienced this loss, but there is no reason why it should not have happened.

**Irrational Belief # 4:** People who harm you or behave badly or unfairly should be severely blamed, reprimanded, and punished for their behavior. They are bad and terrible individuals.

*Rational Alternative Beliefs:* (a) I can tell people firmly and directly that what they are doing has negative consequences for me, but don't have to go so far as to punish them for their behavior. I may feel irritated or hurt, but I don't have to berate that person; (b) Just because I think something is wrong, doesn't mean that it is wrong; (c) I (or others) may have behaved offensively, unfairly, or incompetently, but that doesn't mean that I (or others) always will; (d) I can recognize and admit my own (or others') mistakes and I can work hard to correct or have others correct them or prevent their future occurrence; (e) Although I may dislike my own and others' behavior, it doesn't help to engage in self-blaming or other-blaming. If I can't change either, it is frustrating but not terrible or dreadful; (f) I wish the other person did not behave that way and I don't like what they did, but it does not follow that he or she must not break my rule(s).

**Irrational Belief # 5:** If something seems dangerous or fearsome, you must become terribly occupied with it and upset about it.

*Rational Alternative Beliefs:* (a) It is impossible to prevent a bad event from occurring by worrying about it. Instead of worrying, I can think constructively and problem-solve; (b) In all likelihood, the event will not be as bad as I fear. Even if it is bad, I can stand it even though it will be uncomfortable; (c) It is better to face a danger or fear and render it non-dangerous, and when impossible, accept the inevitable; (d) Worrying about many situations will only aggravate rather than improve them; (e) Although I might be fearful of something in the past, I don't have to be fearful today;

(f) I will try not to exaggerate the importance or significance of things and situations and won't blame or criticize myself for excessive worrying.

**Irrational Belief # 6:** People and things should turn out better than they do and you have to view it as awful and horrible if you do not find perfect solutions to life's hassles.

*Rational Alternative Beliefs:* (a) I do not need to overreact to these pressures. It doesn't appear that a perfect solution exists. I will accept reality and do the best that I can; (b) I will determine my priorities and accomplish what I can by assertively communicating my limits to others; (c) If others are not satisfied, that is unfortunate but not terrible or awful. I can work towards improving the situation.

**Irrational Belief # 7:** Emotional misery comes from external pressure and you have little ability to control your feelings or rid yourself of anxiety, depression, and hostility.

*Rational Alternative Beliefs:* (a) I can stand it when things go wrong and decide whether the situation is intolerable; (b) I do have quite a bit of control over how I react to situations; Others also have choices in how they react to me; (c) I am responsible for my own behavior and can accept reasonable consequences as long as I respect the rights of others. I do not take 100 percent responsibility for how others react to me; (d) When I feel overwhelmed with anxiety, depression, or guilt, I can realize that others and events don't create my feelings but my own irrational thoughts do.

**Irrational Belief # 8:** You will find it easier to avoid facing many of life's difficulties and self-responsibilities than to undertake more rewarding forms of self-discipline.

*Rational Alternative Beliefs:* (a) Even though I get immediate relief when I avoid a frustrating situation or problem, it also turns out to be much less rewarding and more upsetting; (b) What I am avoiding will probably not be as awful as I convince myself it is; (c) Avoidance does not ultimately lead to happiness; (d) The so-called easy way is invariably harder in the long run.

**Irrational Belief # 9:** Your past remains all important and because something or someone once strongly influenced your life, it has to keep determining your feelings and behavior today.

*Rational Alternative Beliefs:* (a) Although my past does have considerable influence, I am not fixed in what I think, feel, or do, and can change; (b) I can learn from my past experiences without clinging to my beliefs about them; (c) Because something might have been true in the past, it is not necessarily true now; (d) I am in control of my own emotional destiny.

**Irrational Belief # 10:** You achieve happiness by inertia and inaction and by passively and noncommittally enjoying yourself.

*Rational Alternative Beliefs:* (a) The more inactive I remain, the more it will block my own needs and goals; (b) Feeling passive and inhibited is unhealthy and can help perpetuate inappropriate negative emotions; (c) We rarely feel happy when inert and inactive; (d) I can decide to involve myself with other people, in feelings, creating things, or in ideas. Finding some persons or activities in which I can honestly get absorbed will help me feel productive and happy.

## Irrational beliefs and our emotions

As you can see, these irrational beliefs or ideas are at the core of virtually all of our emotional upsets. Become familiar with them so that you can associate a particular emotion with the one or more irrational beliefs usually responsible for it. For example, anxiety basically consists of Irrational Belief # 5: *If something seems dangerous or fearsome, you must become terribly occupied with it and upset about it.* While real and rational fears do exist, inappropriate anxiety consists of overconcern and exaggerated fear. It is based on the demand for certainty in our lives and results when we do not get guarantees. Concern is an emotion that is associated with the belief, "I hope this event doesn't happen, but if it does, it would be unfortunate," whereas anxiety occurs when we think, "This must not happen and it would be awful and horrible if it does." Most of what we refer to as anxiety also results from an overconcern for what someone might think about us or the fear of making public mistakes, antagonizing, or losing the approval of others. If you have some fear of disapproval, challenge this fear by showing yourself that while disapproval from others might be uncomfortable, it is not awful or catastrophic. Most negative events turn out to be less horrible than you have anxiously predicted. Unfortunately, overconcern and worrying about situations will usually worsen rather than improve them.

Depression mostly stems from Irrational Belief # 3: *You have to view life as awful, terrible, or catastrophic when you get seriously frustrated, treated unfairly, or rejected.* While you may find it unpleasant or unfortunate when you do not get what you want out of life, it isn't catastrophic or terrible unless you think it is. If you believe "It is very unfortunate that I have experienced this frustrating situation," you will feel appropriately concerned. However, if you think, "This shouldn't have happened. It has to change, otherwise I'll never be happy," you will feel hopeless, depressed, and angry. Anytime you make yourself terribly upset and depressed about your frustrations, you will invariably prevent yourself from achieving your desired goals. If there are some serious frustrations that you cannot change or eliminate, it might be best to accept them. Convince yourself that frustrations and irritations are the norm in life, and that everyone experiences them, and that they do not typically cause a catastrophe.

Anger generally results from Irrational Belief # 4: *People who harm you or behave badly or unfairly should be severely blamed, reprimanded, and punished for their behavior. They are bad and terrible individuals.* When you blame others you are angry and hostile toward them. You are basically saying, "I don't like your behavior and because I don't like it, you shouldn't act that way." Regrettably, problem anger is an emotion which interferes with goal-directed behavior. Even when someone has acted badly or unfairly, it is unlikely that your anger will prevent the behavior from occurring again. When you catch yourself blaming others, look for the unhelpful thinking habits and irrational assumptions behind your anger. When you feel angry and hostile it is likely the result of your perfectionism and demand thinking that others should conform to your rigid and inflexible internal standards. In anger, the person believes that others absolutely must not break the rule and damns them for doing so. If you "dislike" or feel "annoyed" at another person's actions, you will have an appropriate feeling. The next section focuses on scientific thinking as a method of challenging your irrational beliefs and overcoming inappropriate feelings of anxiety, depression, and anger.

## Scientific thinking

The scientific method relies on facts, reality, and logical thinking. It also avoids rigid and all-or-none thinking and readily revises and changes its ideas to accommodate new information. Scientific thinking will help you avoid dogmatic opinion and keep assumptions about yourself and others open to change. If you are consistently scientific and flexible about your desires, preferences, and values, they will not escalate into inappropriate feelings of anxiety, depression, and anger (Ellis, 1988).

In order to think like a scientist, you should ask yourself whether your current thinking is fact or opinion. For example, a fact has evidence to support its truth and is driven by balanced thought. An opinion is based on a personal viewpoint and mostly driven by emotion. If you scientifically question and challenge your irrational beliefs and unhelpful thinking habits, you will see that they are unrealistic, illogical, inflexible, and rigid, and not in your best interest. Realizing that many of your thoughts are opinions rather than fact makes it less likely that you will be distressed by them, and more able to make sensible and calm decisions about the best action to take. Here is a brief example. Imagine that you feel upset because few of your colleagues speak with you, ask you to lunch, or socialize with you. You tell yourself, "Nobody likes me. It is terrible and awful. I feel depressed and worthless." Your depression likely stems from Irrational Belief # 1: *You must—yes, must—have sincere love and approval almost all of the time from people you find significant, and if not, it is awful.* Use scientific thinking to analyze this thought by asking these questions: (a) Is this thought realistic and factual? (b) Is the thought logical and rational? and (c) Is this thought flexible rather than rigid? The answer to all of these questions is no. Clearly, there is no law or rule that says you must be approved and accepted by everyone. In fact, there is a very good possibility that many people will not approve of you. It is certainly not logical because it does not follow that everyone must approve of you in every situation and nearly all of the time. This thought is definitely inflexible in that it holds that everyone should approve and accept you or it is awful and terrible. A more balanced and rational thought might be: "I would like to be socially accepted by all of my colleagues, but I do not need such approval" or "I'm overgeneralizing. While not everyone might like me, I'm sure that there are others who do and that they will enjoy socializing with me." You might also think, "I might find it uncomfortable and inconvenient that my colleagues don't accept me, but it doesn't mean that my life will be awful or catastrophic." So, whenever you feel seriously upset (i.e., inappropriately anxious, depressed, angry) assume that you are thinking unscientifically.

## Disputing exercise

Here is a rational exercise. Think about a time in your life when you felt intensely anxious, depressed, or angry. What were you overconcerned about? Meeting new people? Doing well at work or school? Getting along with a colleague or co-worker? Winning approval from someone you liked? Being treated unfairly? Being ignored by a friend or relative? Remember or imagine the activating event (your A) in which you responded with an intense negative emotional consequence (your C). Ask yourself, "What did I tell myself just before I became upset?" Once you have identified the unrealistic or irrational belief(s) (your iB) that caused this disturbed feeling, use the prompts in Table 5.3 to forcefully challenge, dispute, and debate these thoughts (Ellis and Dryden, 1987, 2007; Vivyan, 2013; Walen et al., 1980). Consciously and deliberately counter each irrational statement with a rational alternative one whether you currently believe it or not. Practice identifying and disputing your irrational beliefs by writing down each question and your answers on the CBT Self-Help Thought Record Form in Appendix G. Assume that every time you feel upset, you are commanding that something go well and that you must have your way. Look for your unhelpful demand thinking musts, shoulds, awfulizing, I-can't-stand-its, and overgeneralizations that caused you to feel inappropriately anxious, depressed, or angry. Check to see whether these feelings appropriately follow your preferences or whether they stem from your unrealistic demands and commands. Ask yourself whether you are turning concern into overconcern, anxiety, depression, or anger. Try to observe the real difference in your thoughts and feelings. Persist until you give up your irrational thoughts and replace them with more balanced and rational alternative ones. Take any of the major irrational beliefs, your shoulds, oughts, musts, and spend at least 15 minutes each day actively and vigorously disputing this belief. It is also important to reward yourself for your efforts. Generate a list of possible self-rewards, ranging from more time in an enjoyed activity to giving yourself a pat on the back, or simply telling yourself, "I've done a good job!" Use these activities as a reinforcer or reward after you have practiced your disputing irrational beliefs exercise each day. Managing our emotions is not always easy or especially enjoyable, and you deserve a reward for your hard work.

TABLE 5.3: DISPUTATION QUESTIONS

| |
|---|
| 1. Is this thought a fact or my opinion? |
| 2. Do I have evidence to support this? Evidence against this? |
| 3. Is this thought flexible rather than rigid? Logical and rational? |
| 4. Is there another, more realistic, way of looking at this situation? |
| 5. Is it really true that I must, should, or have to…? |
| 6. Can I stand it? How have I tolerated these situations in the past? |
| 7. Is this situation really in my control? Is there another explanation other than blaming myself? |
| 8. Am I overgeneralizing from a specific event or occurrence? |
| 9. What's the worse that could realistically happen? How bad would that be? |
| 10. What is a more balanced (rational) alternative belief/ thought? |

# Overcoming your past

Regardless of your background, personal history, or where you are located on the autism spectrum, you have the capacity for self-awareness and the power to control your own emotional destiny. We are not born with specific thoughts, feelings, and behaviors. Nor do our environment or surroundings directly make us act or feel in a certain way. Vigorously challenge Irrational Belief # 7: *Emotional misery comes from external pressure and you have little ability to control your feelings or rid yourself of anxiety, depression, and hostility.* Changing this belief is the cornerstone of CBT (Walen *et al.*, 1980). Unless you assume responsibility for your own feelings and understand that you have created them and can therefore change them, you will continually blame situations, your past, and other people for your emotional upsets. Although our genetic makeup and social background can have a strong influence on our behavior, we have the ability to change our thoughts, feelings, and actions. While it may be helpful to discuss our past experiences and understand how our history might have influenced our lives, CBT mostly focuses on the "here and now" problems and ways to improve your emotional well-being in the present (DeRubeis *et al.*, 2010; Dryden *et al.*, 2010). Understanding your past experiences and how and when you first upset yourself are not critical to overcoming your anxiety and depression. Conventional insight, even when correct, will not tell you what really caused you to become upset or what you can do to overcome it. In fact, it may actually block effective problem-solving (Ellis, 1988).

It is your present system of beliefs and ideas that are important, regardless of where they originated. So, no matter what your past history, or how your parents, teachers or others in your life may have helped you to feel upset, you continue to be upset because of the vicious cycle of unrealistic and irrational thoughts you originally held. Unfortunately, we rarely challenge Irrational Belief # 9: *Your past remains all important and because something once strongly influenced your life, it has to keep determining your feelings and behavior today.* We resist making changes in ourselves because we continue to think about these past experiences and keep reinforcing our old beliefs about these events. Instead of automatically repeating past mistakes, you can calmly observe and question this behavior. If fact, you can use your past for your own present and future benefit by objectively acknowledging your past behavior and developing new ways of thinking. For example, when you feel overwhelmed with anxiety, depression or anger, you can remind yourself that other people and events do not create these feelings and that it is your own illogical, internalized beliefs and thoughts that produce these feelings. Step back and objectively examine your own ideas and beliefs and identify and question them. While it is impossible to change the behavior of others, you have the ability to control and change your own thoughts and behaviors. So, avoid thinking that your past is all important and that because someone or something at one time influenced your life, it must also determine your feelings and behavior today. If you let yourself be strongly influenced by the past, you will stop looking for alternative solutions to your current problems. When you unconditionally accept the influences of your past, you are being unrealistic because the present is significantly different from the past. Remember, a historical basis for your current behavior is no reason for allowing it to continue.

Here is a brief example of how we tend to persist in believing an irrational or unrealistic idea from our past. Suppose when you were in school, you thought that your teachers treated you unfairly which made you feel depressed and worthless. You conclude that if your teachers had been fair and treated you with respect, you wouldn't feel this way. You think that even now some people still treat you unfairly and that you feel dejected and unhappy because as in the past, you are not given the absolute respect you deserve. It is not your school experience that causes you to feel depressed and miserable today. You create your own emotional upset by continuing to think about the same illogical belief you held in the past, thereby upsetting yourself over and over again.

Try this exercise. Think of a traumatic event from your early life or past when you felt intensely depressed or anxious. Next, try to figure out what you told yourself that made the event or situation traumatic or intensely hurtful. Find the unrealistic and irrational thoughts that made you upset as a child or adolescent. Now look for the self-defeating idea that you have kept alive and continue to tell yourself since that time. Use your understanding of the ABCs of emotions to understand exactly how you upset yourself during your childhood or adolescence and how you are still upsetting yourself at the present time. Whenever you think that your early experiences have made you upset today, recall and relive those experiences and find the unhelpful and irrational thoughts that led to your past emotional upset, and notice how you are still clinging to these beliefs today. Keep in mind that the past has passed and it has no automatic effect on your present and future behavior. You can overcome your past and control your own emotional destiny!

## Self-acceptance

Self-acceptance is an important component of CBT (Dryden et al., 2010; Ellis, 1988). Self-acceptance means fully accepting yourself no matter what your traits or how you perform or achieve. It does not mean self-esteem, self-confidence or self-regard. These terms imply that you can accept yourself because you perform or behave in a specific way or because people accept you based on your achievements (Ellis and Harper, 1975). This involves disputing Irrational Belief # 2: *You must prove yourself thoroughly competent, adequate, and achieving at all times, or you must at least have real competence or talent in some important area.* Self-acceptance means that you nonjudgmentally accept yourself for who you are without rating or evaluating yourself or requiring the approval of others. Strive to accept your thoughts, feelings, perceptions, and actions, and use the experience from unfortunate decisions and behaviors to help develop more effective ways of feeling and acting in the future. When we accept ourselves, we also accept and tolerate others.

Self-acceptance also means accepting reality and combating your perfectionism and unhelpful thinking habits by challenging Irrational Belief # 6: *People and things should turn out better than they do and you have to view it as awful and horrible if you do not find perfect solutions to life's hassles.* As human beings, we are fallible and highly imperfect. Demand and all-or-nothing thinking results in self-defeating behavior that invariably leads to feelings of anxiety and depression. The idea that there is an absolute and perfect solution to life's troubles is unrealistic since few things are black and white, and typically there are many alternative solutions to a problem situation. Here are some general ideas for dealing with perfectionism and accepting your personal reality (Ellis, 1988).

- When others behave badly towards you or in relation to themselves, ask yourself whether you should really upset yourself about their behavior. Do their actions truly have a significant effect on your life? Will people change their behavior because you expect or demand that they do so?

- When people act badly towards you, don't severely criticize or judge them. It is unreasonable to think that others must not behave the way they do. Telling yourself that the person or situation is unlikely to change no matter how much you think they should and accept that fact, will keep you from feeling inappropriately angry and resentful. People are independent entities. While we are in control of our own emotional destiny, we do not have control over the behavior of others.

- Continue to fight against your own perfectionism. You will never be perfect and nor will anyone else you know. We are all fallible human beings. The search for absolute certainty and perfection involves the fear of living in an uncertain world and evaluating yourself and others. The result is anxiety and depression. Remember, accept yourself and others for who you and they are.

- Since there are no perfect solutions to problems and difficulties, accept some compromises and reasonable solutions. The more you try to see the bigger picture and objectively observe both sides of an issue, the more likely you are to find the best logical answer to a problem.

## Low frustration tolerance

This is a good point to discuss low frustration tolerance (LFT). Low frustration tolerance usually stems from our demand thinking. For example, you might think that people must give you exactly what you want and conditions must always meet your expectations. If not, it is awful and you won't tolerate or stand for it. In other words, your life should be easy and others should give you what you want in order to be happy. Or, you might lack persistence and self-discipline and think that it is just too difficult to dispute your irrational beliefs and that overcoming your emotional upsets should be much easier (Dryden *et al.*, 2010; Ellis, 1988). You may also find yourself procrastinating and clinging to Irrational Belief # 8: *You will find it easier to avoid facing many of life's difficulties and self-responsibilities than to undertake more rewarding forms of self-discipline.* Why is it important to recognize LFT? Because no matter how well you understand the ABCs of emotions and dispute your unhelpful thoughts and irrational beliefs, yet give in to your anxiety, depression, and anger, rather than making a strong effort to overcome them, you are a victim of LFT. Likewise, when you temporarily make yourself less anxious, depressed, or angry but then give up any further effort, you are engaging in LFT. Unfortunately, some people prefer their "comfortable discomfort" and the status quo to the inconvenience of vigorously disputing their irrational ideas and working toward emotional change. How do you reduce LFT? Understanding the ABCs of emotions and how to dispute one's irrational beliefs and cognitive distortions is simply not enough to achieve lasting change. Because LFT stems from the idea that working to overcome your emotional problems should not require persistence and effort, you will not improve unless you seriously accept the fact that it requires hard work and practice to actively change your irrational thoughts and strongly act against them. Use the rational statements shown in Table 5.4 to refocus your CBT efforts and help combat your LFT (Hauck, 1980). Vigorously challenge Irrational Belief # 10: *You achieve happiness by inertia and inaction and by passively and noncommittally enjoying yourself.* Although inactivity may reduce the apprehension and fear of meeting new people, it will keep you from developing different perspectives and leave you feeling socially isolated and lonely. Likewise, your restricted and solitary activities will actually decrease enjoyment over time because a sense of personal accomplishment and satisfaction comes from making commitments and involving other people who are important to you. Feeling inert, passive, and inhibited will only help perpetuate your inappropriate feelings of anxiety and depression (Ellis and Harper, 1975).

TABLE 5.4: RATIONAL STATEMENTS

| |
|---|
| 1. The more a person blames himself or herself for unacceptable behavior, the more unacceptable behavior that person will perform. |
| 2. Self-blame distracts the person's attention from focusing on a solution to problem. |
| 3. If people are truly imperfect, it does not make sense that they can behave perfectly. |
| 4. Life is frequently unfair. |

| 5. Not getting one's way is frustrating, but not awful and tragic. |
| --- |
| 6. Compulsively striving for perfection is really self-defeating. |
| 7. People have the right to be wrong. |
| 8. Very few events or situations in life are truly catastrophic. |
| 9. There are no bad people in the world, only bad behavior. |
| 10. Obsessively focusing on a problem usually increases it. |

## Self-management

Once you have successfully challenged your irrational thoughts and developed a range of healthier feelings, you may consider using self-management each week to monitor your progress with CBT. Self-management involves evaluating and recording your emotions and use of skills. The objective is to be aware of and regulate your own behavior so as to require no assistance or reminders from others. The activity of focusing attention on one's own behavior and self-recording these observations can have a positive "reactive" effect and keep you in touch with your feelings, reinforce your skills, and prevent a relapse. This will help you become more independent, self-reliant, and responsible. Self-management can be conducted when and where it is convenient for you. For example, set aside 10 to 15 minutes each week to check your mood and progress. Use the Daily Mood and Thought Worksheet in Appendix H to record your thoughts and emotions, and rate the intensity of your mood during both the current and past weeks. Use the following questions as a self-management guide (Cully and Teten, 2008).

- Did I use any of the tools I learned from CBT this week? If not, what problem did I have this week that could have been helped through the use of these strategies?

- How will I remember to use the tools next time?

- What positive things happened this week? How did I make those good things happen?

- What problems can occur before my next self-management time?

- What CBT skills can I use to deal with these problems?

- How can I think about these problems in a different way?

- What can I do to change the feelings associated with these problems?

## Summary

As we have seen, feelings of anxiety, depression, and anger are not caused by your autistic traits or condition, but rather originate in some irrational beliefs about specific situations and events in your life. You learned that while the past influences people to repeat old patterns of behavior, it does not have to exert an overwhelming influence on your life and that you are in control of your own emotional future. You also learned the importance of self-acceptance and dealing with your perfectionism. Your job now is to put what you have learned into practice. If you continue to challenge and dispute the basic unrealistic ideas with which you disturb yourself, you will see clearly the lack of logic behind these beliefs and on the basis of better information and healthier thinking, change the notions that cause and maintain your cycle of emotional upsets. Remember, when something unfortunate happens to you, you should feel concerned, appropriately sad, disappointed, sorry, regretful, frustrated, or annoyed. Not overconcerned and inappropriately anxious, depressed, or enraged. Persist at using the scientific method of questioning and challenging your cognitive distortions and irrational beliefs until you begin to give them up. Practice! Practice! Practice! Although practice will not make you perfect, it will increase your effectiveness and help you learn new ways of thinking, feeling, and behaving which will lead to a more satisfying and less stressful life. In the next chapter, we will discuss some additional techniques that will help you cope and manage the emotional distress in your life.

**Answers to the iB and rB exercise:**

1. rB, 2. iB, 3. iB, 4. rB, 5. iB, 6. rB, 7. iB, 8. rB, 9. iB, 10. rB

# CHAPTER 6

# IMAGERY, MINDFULNESS, AND SELF-TALK

In addition to disputing and challenging irrational beliefs and unhelpful thinking habits, CBT employs other methods to help you cope with anxiety and depression. In this chapter, you will learn about imagery, mindfulness, and self-talk. We will also discuss problem-solving as a strategy for dealing more effectively with the stressful problems of daily living.

## Imagery

Mental imagery is a technique that can be used in CBT to ease stress and promote an overall sense of well-being. Imagery focuses on increasing cognitive, emotional, and physical control by changing the focus of our thoughts. We have all had the experience of daydreaming about pleasant events or situations that have made us feel calm and relaxed. Imagery uses much the same process to distract us from our everyday problems and help reduce stress. Imagery can also be an effective strategy for visualizing new more adaptive ways of coping with feelings of depression and anxiety (Dryden *et al.*, 2010; Ellis, 1988; Ellis and Dryden, 1987, 2007).

## Guided Imagery

Imagery uses the power of the brain, images and the perception that you are either somewhere else or in a different state of mind, to enhance pleasant experiences and promote psychological well-being. Imagery helps reduce stress, tension, and anxiety by changing your thoughts and emotions through distraction. Guided imagery is a technique in which you imagine the sights and sounds of a relaxing scene or series of pleasant experiences. The most common mental picture usually involves a tropical beach, warm sun, and the soothing sounds of the ocean. The type of scene is not important; what matters most is that you imagine every sight, sound and smell and transport yourself to that place.

Here is a generic example of a guided imagery exercise. Begin your visualization by getting comfortable in a quiet place where you won't be disturbed, and take a couple of minutes to focus on your breathing. Close your eyes and become aware of any area of your body where there is tension, and let that tension go with each exhalation. Once your entire body feels relaxed, travel to your favorite place. This place is calm and secure. There are no worries here. Take a moment to fully experience your favorite place. What do you see? Hear? Smell? Stroll around and take in all the pleasing things there are to see. Feel the air around you and relax. The air is fresh and easy to breathe. Notice how your body feels. Say to yourself, "I am relaxed here. This place is special and makes me feel calm and peaceful." While in your tranquil and secure place, you might choose to give it a name, either a word or phrase that you can use to bring this image back, whenever you want to. When you are done visiting this special place, open your eyes and stay in a comfortable position. Continue to breathe easily, in a relaxed and regular way. Take as long as you want to enjoy this sensation. Feel comfortable in knowing that your special place is always available to you, and that you will feel relaxed, even after you leave. Create your own personal guided imagery script and visit your special place whenever you feel anxious, stressed or need to relax.

You can also use your strong visualization ability to help cope with feelings of anxiety, depression, and anger. For example, picture in detail the feeling and behavior you would like to experience, in what situation and with whom. For depression, in your mind's eye, see yourself feeling hopeful and doing and enjoying the things you used to do or would like to do. For anxiety, imagine yourself coping in a situation where you felt highly anxious. See yourself persisting and following the situation or task through to a successful completion. For anger, visualize yourself handling a situation in a calm, non-aggressive but assertive way, respecting the rights and opinions of others. Use different scenarios for each situation and rehearse each scenario in your imagination, using the desired behaviors. Anticipate others' responses and practice responding to them in different ways. Picture yourself appearing composed and positive. Imagine what that looks like, what you will be doing, and how you will be doing it. As with all imagery exercises, it is helpful to strengthen the image by thinking about each of our senses, noticing even small details in what we can see and hear. You might also prepare a script of what you want to say in each situation and practice this imagery activity several times a day. The more you practice, the easier it will become, and the easier you will find it to cope when an actual situation occurs. You will also find that using imagery can help disrupt the cycle of negative thinking and result in more positive, healthier feelings.

## Rational imagery exercise

Rational imagery is a relatively easy yet very effective way to reduce your emotional distress through your ability to imagine. Rational imagery will allow you to practice changing your inappropriate negative emotions to more healthy and appropriate ones. Here is an imagery exercise that will help you to think more rationally and make yourself less emotionally upset (Ellis, 1988). Use your knowledge of the ABCs of emotions presented in Chapter 4 and picture yourself or imagine as intensely as you can, the details of some unpleasant activating (A) experience that has happened to you or might likely occur in the future. Let yourself feel noticeably uncomfortable and upset; anxious, depressed, or angry, at C (your emotional consequence). Get in touch with this disturbed feeling and let yourself intensely experience it for a short time. Don't try to avoid this feeling. As you feel upset at C, notice what you keep telling yourself at B (your belief system) to make yourself feel upset. When you clearly identify these irrational beliefs, vigorously dispute (D) them with the scientific thinking and logic discussed in the previous chapter. Strongly imagine how you would feel and behave after you have substituted these thoughts with appropriate and rational alternative beliefs about your activating (A) experience. Intensely picture yourself believing your alternative rational ideas about A and feeling appropriately concerned rather than anxious, depressed, or angry at C. Keep practicing so that you first imagine a negative event or something unpleasant; then make yourself feel anxious, depressed, or hostile about this image. Notice the irrational beliefs (iBs) you hold that create your emotional upset; then work on changing these irrational beliefs. Practice this same process, over and over again until you can easily picture yourself successfully disputing these ideas and beliefs and acting in accordance with your new rational ideas which result in concern, annoyance, and disappointment, rather than feelings of anxiety, depression, and hostility. You can use this rational imagery technique before an unpleasant or upsetting event occurs. It can also be done at the same time the negative event is taking place or an hour later, or even a day or two later. If you practice this imagery technique at least once (preferably two or three times) every day for the next few weeks, you will reach the point where whenever you think of the same or similar type of upsetting event, or when it actually occurs in your life, you will more easily and automatically feel displeased and disappointed rather than inappropriately upset. Don't give up. Remember, you create and control your feelings. You can change them!

## Illustrative example

Suppose that you are concerned about being embarrassed, ridiculed, and rejected at a large social gathering (at A, the activating event or experience). You feel anxious, depressed, and self-downing about this (at C, your emotional consequence) and want to get over this disturbed feeling. Imagine the details of this situation, the people, place, sounds and so forth. Let yourself feel, as you visualize the circumstances of being embarrassed and humiliated, intensely depressed and worthless for a short time. Now actively look for the irrational beliefs (at B) with which you created your disturbed feelings. Persist until you identify these inappropriate beliefs, especially the shoulds, oughts, and musts. For example, you will probably find that your irrational beliefs include: "I must have approval and acceptance from all of the people I find significant," "I must be thoroughly competent and adequate in all my activities," "I find it awful to be criticized and rejected and can't stand it," and "If this happens, it proves that I am socially inept and will never be accepted by others." Identify your irrational beliefs and then vigorously and persistently dispute (D) them until you no longer believe them to be true. Picture yourself holding new, appropriate and rational ideas about your activating (A) experience. For example, you will now think "I would like to be approved of by every significant person, but I do not need such approval" or "If I am not successful, I will likely be unhappy, but not depressed and miserable," or "I can stand it when things go wrong and have considerable control over how I react to situations." As you picture yourself internalizing these new rational alternative beliefs, see yourself responding appropriately to your negative activating (A) experience by accepting yourself completely, assuming responsibility for your own behavior and the practical consequences, regardless of how unsuccessful you may be in social situations, and finding others with whom you enjoy socializing. Practice this rational imagery several times each day until the image of social failure easily and automatically produces feelings of disappointment and regret, rather than anxiety, depression, and feelings of inadequacy.

## Mindfulness

Mindfulness strategies can also be incorporated into CBT to help reduce stress and promote acceptance (Fruzzetti and Erikson, 2010). Mindfulness is a state of awareness or presence of mind. Mindfulness simply means paying attention in a particular way, intentionally, in the present moment, and nonjudgmentally to internal and external events. Internal events include one's thoughts, emotions, perceptions, and body sensations. External events include a person's surroundings, situations, and interpersonal experiences. Mindfulness generally involves a heightened awareness of the senses such as noticing one's breathing or feeling the sensation of one's body and being in the here and now. Mindfulness is a practical way to notice thoughts, physical sensations, sights, sounds, and smells, and anything we might not usually observe because we are too focused on the future or the past; thinking about what we need to do or mulling over what we should have or should not have done. We have all had the experience of driving a car for miles on what seems to be automatic pilot, without really being aware of what we are doing or how we got to our destination. In the same way, we may not be really present, moment-by-moment, for a good part of our lives. We can often be miles away or lost in our thoughts without realizing it. It is during these times that we are the most vulnerable to reacting to stressful situations. Internal events, thoughts, feelings, and sensations (of which we may be only vaguely aware) can easily trigger our unhelpful thinking habits and negatively affect our mood. Becoming more conscious of our thoughts, feelings, and body sensations, from moment to moment, allows us greater emotional freedom and choice. In other words, we do not have stay in the same old psychological rut that may have caused us problems in the past.

Although mindfulness might appear to be a relatively simple activity, it is very different from how we usually think. Mindfulness focuses on becoming aware of all incoming thoughts and feelings and accepting them, but not attaching or reacting to them. For example, when we become depressed, we return to our automatic negative thoughts and irrational beliefs which can trigger an intense emotional reaction. Mindfulness helps interrupt this automatic process by focusing less on reacting to incoming events, and instead, accepting and observing them without judging them. Practicing mindfulness allows you to notice when these automatic thoughts are occurring and to adjust your reaction to be more of a reflection. Even the most distressing sensations, feelings, thoughts, and experiences, can then be viewed from a wider perspective as passing events in your mind, rather than automatically true. This allows you to distance yourself from your thoughts and develop a more balanced perspective. As you become more experienced at using mindfulness, you will learn to be aware of your thoughts and feelings, to become an observer, and consequently, more accepting. This will result in less stressful feelings and increase your ability to manage your emotions effectively.

## Distancing your thoughts

Distancing your thoughts involves acknowledging the thought as a thought, not reacting automatically, and then choosing to focus your attention somewhere else. Consider your thoughts as temporary images, sensations, or words, rather than the statements of fact that we usually accept them to be (our unhelpful thinking habits). We can learn to simply observe these words, images or sensations, rather than engage or accept them. The following questions will help distance yourself from your thoughts (Vivyan, 2013):

- What is happening right now? What thoughts, feelings, and sensations do I notice?

- What am I reacting to? What meaning am I giving to this event?

- What is the result of my believing this thought? Not believing this thought?

- Am I evaluating this situation? How might I describe it instead?

- Is this a thought, feeling, sensation, or a memory from the past?

- Am I predicting what might happen in the future?

- Is this one of those unhelpful thinking habits? (see Chapter 4)

Although we tend to fight against our distressing thoughts and feelings, in some situations it might be best to just notice them and give up the struggle. In other words, we can acknowledge and accept them and then focus on another more helpful thought. Unfortunately, there are some situations we just can't change. When you face considerable frustration and there seems no way to overcome or control it, it is best to realistically (and rationally) accept it. As discussed in the previous chapter, this means viewing these situations as disappointing, unfortunate, and regrettable, and not terrible, awful, and catastrophic. So, when you are confronted with real-life situations you cannot change, you will do well to practice what might be called sensation—neglect or distraction. Deliberately distracting yourself with another, more pleasant thought or activity often proves to be more effective (Ellis, 1988).

## Mindful activities

Here is a relatively easy mindfulness activity. Walking is something most of us do at some time during the day. Even if for a short time, you can practice mindful walking. Take a walk and spend time just looking, listening, and noticing. Rather than thinking, look around and notice what you see, hear, and sense. Become aware of the sensations in your own body, your breathing and the movement of your feet, legs, arms, head and body as you take each step. When thoughts intrude, just notice them, and then bring your attention back to your walking. The more you practice, the more you might notice your thoughts interfering, but that is to be expected. The only aim of this mindful exercise is to consistently bring your attention back to the activity of walking and noticing sensations, both around and within you.

Mindful breathing is also something that you can do almost anytime throughout the day. Take a moment right now and try this activity. Look at your watch and note the time. For the next 60 seconds your task is to focus all of your attention on your breathing. Leave your eyes open and breathe normally. Be prepared to catch your mind drifting off (because it will) and return your attention to your breathing whenever it does so. Once again, it is normal for thoughts to happen, and for your attention to follow them. When thoughts, emotions, physical sensations, or external sounds do occur, simply acknowledge them, let them come and go without judging or reacting to them. No matter how many times this happens, just keep bringing your attention back to your breathing. Over time, you can gradually extend the duration of this exercise into longer and longer periods. The primary goal is to achieve calm, nonjudging awareness and acceptance, allowing thoughts and feelings to come and go without getting caught up in them. Try this mindfulness breathing activity at least once each day for the next several weeks.

## Self-talk

As discussed in Chapter 3, we all tend to fall into some unhelpful thinking habits and think negatively about ourselves and situations at times. We also frequently engage in negative self-talk. Self-talk refers to our inner voice or the thoughts that go on inside everyone's head. Most often we don't even realize that we are having conversations with ourselves. Self-talk can be positive, negative, or neutral. It can be an interpretation of your feelings and how you perceive a certain situation. It may also be based on your own personal observations or feedback you get from other individuals. Unfortunately, when self-talk is negative, it produces negative feelings such as anxiety and depression. In fact, self-talk can create its own reality and positively or negatively affect many aspects of our lives. For example, negative self-talk is usually associated with a corresponding negative outcome while positive self-talk mostly results in a desirable effect. Telling yourself you can do something can actually help it happen. Telling yourself you can't do something can also make that become a reality.

If you are a negative self-talker, you are likely unaware of it. Thinking the worst can be second nature after many years of doing it. It also tends to become pronounced and intense during stressful situations. Likewise, overthinking a situation can exaggerate your negative self-talk by replaying a negative event or focusing on your own weaknesses and shortcomings. Negative feelings actually tend to get worse the more attention you give them. You continue to hear your inner voice doubting, blaming, or comparing yourself to others. The more you focus on negative events or shortcomings, the harder it is to put them behind you. Self-talk can also determine how you relate to yourself and how you appear to other people. For example, suppose that you are uncomfortable in social groups and think that you have nothing interesting to say to others. If you keep telling yourself this, other people will be inclined to perceive you that way as well. People who think negatively tend to be less outgoing and have weaker social networks than positive thinkers.

Unlike most external factors, self-talk is within each individual's control. One strategy is to identify and gradually alter the flow of your self-talk. This can be particularly helpful in altering depressive thought patterns and coping with stress and anxiety. When you are feeling stressed, depressed, or anxious, take this as a cue to listen to your self-talk. Identify the feeling and then ask yourself, "What was I saying to myself right before I started feeling this way?" "Are my conversations positive and affirming or the opposite?" Write down your thoughts and analyze the statements and the feelings behind them. Use the Self-Talk Record Form in Appendix I to take an inventory of your self-talk and list the types of conversations you have with yourself. As soon as possible after an event or experience, write down what you said to yourself under the appropriate columns. In the "Situation" column, write down what you were doing and what was going on around you at the time. Pay special attention to when you are feeling calm or upset to see how your thoughts differ at these times. Keep an ongoing record of your internal positive and negative conversations. Although it takes time, this is one of the best ways to assess your self-talk.

Whenever you fall into a pattern of negative self-talk, stop and take the time to challenge and dispute (as in the previous chapter) that point of view. Stop and think of at least three positive alternatives, and from these, choose one that seems the most balanced and rational. This positive alternative outcome is evidence that your current negative perspective is distorted and unrealistic. Likewise, don't say anything to yourself that you wouldn't say to a best friend or valued colleague. If you catch yourself in a cycle of negative self-talk, ask yourself, "Would I say this to _____?" Don't let this dialogue pass without defending yourself against your own negative voice. Learn to practice assertive optimism. Assertive optimism is seeing people, events, and situations from a positive perspective. Thinking in a positive way and disrupting a negative thinking pattern is a good strategy to use to when experiencing a stressful situation.

## Positive self-statements

Using positive statements can help us develop a new attitude toward ourselves and counteract negative automatic thoughts. Choose a statement from Table 6.1, adapt one, or make up one that has specific meaning for you (Vivyan, 2013). Repeat, repeat, and repeat this positive self-talk throughout the day, every day, of every week, of every month. Notice that these positive statements are also rational alternative thoughts. Listen to your inner voice and whenever you notice that you are engaging in negative self-talk, immediately interrupt the conversation with a positive self-statement. You might also want to make or print out a card with your positive self-statements, and carry it with you.

TABLE 6.1: POSITIVE SELF-STATEMENTS

| |
|---|
| 1.  I am determined and successful. |
| 2.  I am a good and worthwhile person. |
| 3.  I have inner strength and resources. |
| 4.  I am confident and competent. |
| 5.  People like me—I am a likeable person and I like myself. |
| 6.  I care about others, I am needed and worthwhile. |
| 7.  I am in control of my life and emotional destiny. |
| 8.  I am in control of my choices. |
| 9.  I have many options and can make rational decisions. |
| 10.  The past has passed. I will take notice of the positive things the present has to offer. |

You can also use positive coping statements during those times when you feel overwhelmed by stressful thoughts and emotions.

We have all lived through some very difficult circumstances, and we can use those experiences to help us through our current problems. We can repeat these encouraging words to ourselves whenever we experience or anticipate an intensely upsetting event or situation. The following are some examples of positive coping statements (Vivyan, 2013).

- Thoughts are just thoughts—they're not necessarily true or factual.

- I have done this before, and I can do it again.

- This is the anxiety I thought I would feel; it's a reminder for me to cope.

- Don't worry; worry won't help anything.

- This is difficult and uncomfortable, but it's only temporary.

- I can use my coping skills and get through this; I am in control.

- It's okay to feel this way, it's a normal reaction.

Use the Coping Thought Worksheet in Appendix J to write down a coping thought or positive statement for each difficult or distressing situation you encounter. You can also complete this activity prior to a situation you anticipate will be especially upsetting for you. Rational coping cards can also be a helpful way of managing difficult situations. Rational coping cards are 3 x 5 inch note cards that you can keep nearby in a desk drawer, pocket, purse, or posted on a mirror or refrigerator. Write one of your major irrational beliefs from the last chapter on one side and its rational alternative on the other. Read them both on a regular basis (e.g., three times a day) and as needed. This will help you cope with problematic situations when they arise and remind you how to cope with a particular irrational thought (Ellis and Dryden, 1987).

## Problem-solving

We live a complex social world. We affect others in our environment (e.g., family, friends, colleagues, co-workers, neighbors, acquaintances) and they influence us. Living in a complicated social environment creates many day-to-day problems for all of us. As you encounter these practical life problems, you will likely experience many intense feelings and emotions about these issues. Once you have learned to dispute your irrational beliefs, achieve more balanced thinking, and develop effective coping skills, you will create more emotional distance and can think more realistically about these problems. At this point, you can use a rational problem-solving approach to identify effective ways of coping with many of the practical problems encountered in everyday living. Problem-solving strategies can be used with a wide range of problems, including anxiety, depression, anger and stress management, and relationship/family difficulties (D'Zurilla and Nezu, 2010). The overall objective of problem-solving is to help you develop confidence in your own ability to deal with life's daily challenges. Problem-solving is an especially good strategy to use to develop a plan for brainstorming solutions for undesirable and unexpected situations that might seem overwhelming and unmanageable (Gaus, 2007). The key to effective problem-solving is to identify constructive goals and avoid destructive goals. This includes potential positive outcomes, as well as limitations and self-defeating consequences of other alternatives. The rational problem-solving approach involves a specific set of steps for analyzing a problem, identifying options for coping, evaluating the options, developing and implementing the plan or solution, and evaluating the outcome(s) (Cully and Teten, 2008; D'Zurilla and Nezu, 2010; Gaus, 2007; Vivyan, 2013). The following questions will help orient you to a problem-solving mindset:

- What is the problem?

- What are all the things I could do about it?

- What will probably happen if I do those things?

- Which solutions do I think will work best?

- After I have tried it, how did I do?

The Problem-Solving Worksheet in Appendix K is designed to guide you through the steps to identify and solve some of the practical problems you might encounter. Once you have identified a specific problem and completed this worksheet, you can refer to it later when faced with similar situations and problems. Actively considering the pros and cons of each potential solution is especially important. Often, writing down options, together with listing the advantages and disadvantages, can be helpful to the problem-solving process. Writing allows additional thoughts, as well as a visual image of your options. Consider solutions in a logical (and rational) manner, so as not to spend a great deal of time agonizing over the problem. You can also "rank order" the solutions based on which are most practical and realistic. During the problem-solving process you might identify some additional irrational beliefs or unhelpful thoughts that might benefit from changes using the disputation techniques reviewed earlier. Return to the ABCs of CBT to deal with any lingering emotional problems that may be blocking your goals. In fact, you can move back and forth between challenging your irrational beliefs and problem-solving efforts.

## Summary

In this chapter we discussed how imagery, mindfulness, positive self-talk, and problem-solving can be used in CBT to help reduce stress and cope with anxiety and depression. You were introduced to guided imagery techniques and learned how they can help you deal with stress, think more rationally, and visualize new ways of coping with your emotional upsets. You learned that mindfulness can be used to increase emotional control and cope with negative experiences by changing the focus of your thoughts. In addition, we discussed how to listen to your inner voice and combat your negative self-talk and thoughts with positive statements. You also discovered how problem-solving can be an effective strategy for managing your emotions and coping with the stressful problems of everyday living. Adding imagery, mindfulness, self-talk, and problem-solving strategies to your self-help CBT "tool box" will help you to relax, improve your mood, reduce stress, and change your thinking for the better. In the next chapter, we will discuss how to maintain the emotional and behavioral gains you've made thus far.

CHAPTER 7

# MAINTAINING YOUR CHANGES

This chapter provides you with a review of important topics from previous chapters and several strategies to enhance and maintain your emotional and behavioral improvements. Emotional change is an ongoing process. You should commit yourself to working toward the internalization of new, rational ways of thinking and feeling by continuing to practice the CBT insights, objectives, and strategies outlined in this book. Regardless of your autistic traits or where you might be situated on the autism spectrum, you can overcome your inappropriate feelings of anxiety, depression, and anger. The following insights will help you to stay focused and maintain your emotional gains (Ellis, 1988; Ellis and Dryden, 1987, 2007).

- *Practice the ABCs of emotions.* Remember, you largely choose to upset yourself about the negative activating events in your life. You mainly feel the way you think. When negative things happen to you at point A, you consciously (or unconsciously) select irrational beliefs and unhelpful thoughts that lead to upsetting consequences (anxiety, depression, and anger). Your past and present situations might affect you, but they do not cause you to be upset. Your thoughts create your emotional upsets.

- *Give up the notion that your past continues to be all important and that because something (or someone) once strongly influenced your life, this must continue without end.* While considering your past history, do your best to learn valuable lessons from it and appreciate that your present will be tomorrow's past, and working to change the present will allow you to build a much better future. Changing your past assumptions and unhelpful thinking habits can help minimize most of the negative influences from your childhood and adolescence. You can overcome your past and rewrite your personal history.

- *Continue to strongly dispute the belief that you must feel accepted by every significant person for nearly everything that you do.* Rather, keep the approval of others as desirable, but not an essential goal. Seriously consider other people's criticisms of your traits without agreeing with their negative evaluations of you. Strive to do what you really enjoy rather than what other people think you must or should do.

- *Surrender the belief that you must perform competently in every situation.* Continue to dispute the assumption that you must always please others and achieve perfectly. Avoid the tendency to evaluate yourself and accept failure as undesirable but not awful or catastrophic. Accept compromise and reasonable rather than absolute and perfect solutions to life's problems.

- *Identify and challenge your unhelpful thinking habits of demand thinking and personalizing, and try to keep from engaging in needless conflict with others.* Do not confuse people with their actions and behavior. Consistently work on accepting yourself and try to remain uniquely you. Involve yourself with others and activities because you actually receive satisfaction from them. Remember, living in a social group involves consideration of other members of your group and when you possess rational self-interest (rather than irrational self-centeredness), you generally find satisfaction in helping and interacting with other people.

- *Dispute the irrational belief that situations or events must be viewed as terrible, horrible, and awful when they do not go the way you want them to go.* When you cannot change them, try to accept them. The greater your frustration, the more you should view it as undesirable, but not intolerable or unbearable.

- *Abandon the idea that if something appears perilous or fearsome, you must become terribly anxious and preoccupied about it.* It is impossible to prevent a negative event from happening by worrying about it. Likewise, worrying about many situations will only worsen rather than improve them.

- *Continue thinking rational alternative beliefs, coping statements, and positive self-talk.* Don't merely repeat these statements or mimic them; carefully think about them as often as possible and frequently throughout the day. Use mindfulness activities to alter your focus of attention and reduce stress, and rational imagery techniques to build on your disputation skills and scientific thinking.

- *Remind yourself that you can change your irrational beliefs by effectively using the scientific method.* With scientific thinking, you will see that your irrational beliefs and unhelpful thinking habits are only assumptions and not facts. You can logically and realistically dispute and change them.

- *Understanding these rational insights is simply not enough.* There is no quick and easy way to change your irrational thoughts and unhelpful ways of thinking, feeling, and behaving. You will only overcome your anxiety and depression and achieve lasting change through hard work, determination, and practice!

## Dealing with relapse

Unfortunately, there will be times in which you will relapse and return to those all too familiar feelings of inappropriate anxiety, depression, and anger. Common thoughts might include: "I shouldn't be feeling this way;" "This means I'm not getting better;" "This is hopeless. I'll always feel depressed;" or "CBT doesn't work for me." Remember that lapses are normal and can be overcome. They happen to almost everyone who at first improves emotionally. So, don't criticize yourself or feel self-defeated if you do backslide. View it as part of being an imperfect human being. Remember our discussion about self-acceptance and resist rating yourself. If you do experience a setback, return to Chapters 4 and 5 and review the strategies you might need to improve upon. You might also use these relapse-prevention sentences: (a) "When I feel (symptom), I will (tool learned in CBT)" and (b) "If _ (stressor) ____, I will (tool learned in CBT)." Use the Maintaining Change Worksheet in Appendix L to remind yourself of what helps most, and what you need to keep practicing. Know when you are most vulnerable to having a setback (e.g., during times of stress or change), and you'll be less likely to have one. It also helps to make a list of warning signs (e.g., more anxious thoughts, feeling down, irritability) that tell you when your anxiety, depression, and anger might be increasing to an inappropriate level. Once you know what your warning signs or "red flags" are, you can then make an action plan to cope with them. You can also use the imagery techniques discussed in the last chapter to deal with any emotional reaction you may experience from having a relapse and falling back to your negative feelings. Use rational imagery to feel only disappointed with a setback and not overconcerned or self-defeated. You can also use coping self-statements such as "I don't like falling back and feeling upset with myself, but I can stand it and will try again."

Keep looking for, discovering, and disputing your irrational beliefs which are upsetting you. Don't fool yourself into believing that if you simply change your language you will always change your thinking. Revisit your internal scientist and forcefully dispute and challenge your irrational beliefs. Get in touch with your inappropriate feelings of anxiety, depression and anger and work on them until you only feel concerned, sorry, regretful, and annoyed. Whenever you feel needlessly upset or dejected, acknowledge that you are having a common but unhealthy feeling and that you (not your autistic traits or someone else) have caused it yourself by engaging in some unhelpful thinking habits and irrational beliefs. Think in terms of preferences rather than absolute musts, shoulds and have tos. Realize that you are quite capable of changing your inappropriate thoughts into appropriate and preferential ones.

## Practice! Practice! Practice!

Keep practicing your CBT skills. If you practice regularly, you'll be in a better position to deal with whatever situations you are likely to face now and in the future. You are also less likely to slide back into old unhelpful thinking habits if you're continually working on new and different ways of overcoming your anxiety, depression, and anger. Schedule a self-management time each week to stay in touch with your feelings and review the skills you've used and need to work on in the future. Practice won't make perfect (no one is), but it will help develop and maintain helpful and balanced thinking habits. Remember and practice the helpful steps you have learned over and over, and even when you feel you can use them effectively, keep practicing so that when you really need those skills, they will come easier to you. After a while, you will more easily notice your thoughts and reactions, realize what you are reacting to, and the meaning you are giving to situations. You will also naturally start to see the bigger picture. Questioning and recognizing different perspectives will help improve your ability to predict and understand the intentions and behavior of others. You can also generalize from your past successes with CBT strategies and use similar techniques to overcome new aspects of your emotional challenges. Once you have used CBT to reduce one part of your psychological discomfort, ask yourself how you can use it again to deal with other stressful situations and circumstances.

Continue to practice the self-help techniques learned from this book until they become second nature for you to use in other areas of your emotional life. Remember, unless you put these techniques and strategies to the test of practice, the effect will not be meaningful or long lasting. Will they absolutely ensure that you will live a stress-free life with no emotional upsets? No. As mentioned earlier in this book, there are some important factors and situations which remain beyond your control. While much of your emotional discomfort cannot be completely eliminated or avoided, you will, with thought and much effort, significantly improve and overcome most of your inappropriate anxiety and depression. Remember, when you feel seriously upset about something that has happened to you, immediately acknowledge your contribution to the problems and use the CBT techniques outlined in this self-help guide to more effectively manage your emotions and improve your psychological well-being. If you intelligently organize and discipline your thinking and your behavior, and follow the basic principles discussed here, it is possible to live a self-fulfilling and emotionally satisfying life in a highly irrational social, world. If after making a determined effort to question and change your own irrational beliefs and self-defeating behavior, your anxiety, depression, or anger continues to seriously interfere with your adaptability, you should seek the help of a mental health professional.

## Epilogue

We have come to the end of our journey. I hope this book has helped you internalize a new way of looking at yourself, at others, and at the world, so that you are now able to more effectively

MAINTAINING YOUR CHANGES | 101

manage your emotions and cope with the negative events in your life. Return to the book frequently. Continue to practice and use the techniques discussed in this text until they can be completed naturally and automatically without thinking. Regardless of your autistic traits or autism spectrum condition, using the CBT techniques and strategies presented in this self-help guide will help you maximize your individuality, freedom, self-control, self-interest, and independence. Remember, no matter what the circumstance, you can choose to feel one way or another about it. You are in control of your own emotional destiny!

# THE ADULT AUTISM SPECTRUM QUOTIENT (AQ) TEST

Below is a list of statements. Please read each statement very carefully and rate how strongly you agree or disagree with it by circling your answer. Please answer all items.

| | | | | | |
|---|---|---|---|---|---|
| 1. | I prefer to do things with others rather than on my own. | definitely agree | slightly agree | slightly disagree | definitely disagree |
| 2. | I prefer to do things the same way over and over again. | definitely agree | slightly agree | slightly disagree | definitely disagree |
| 3. | If I try to imagine something, I find it very easy to create a picture in my mind. | definitely agree | slightly agree | slightly disagree | definitely disagree |
| 4. | I frequently get so strongly absorbed in one thing that I lose sight of other things. | definitely agree | slightly agree | slightly disagree | definitely disagree |
| 5. | I often notice small sounds when others do not. | definitely agree | slightly agree | slightly disagree | definitely disagree |
| 6. | I usually notice car number plates or similar strings of information. | definitely agree | slightly agree | slightly disagree | definitely disagree |

| | |  |  |  |  |
|---|---|---|---|---|---|
| 7. | Other people frequently tell me that what I've said is impolite, even though I think it is polite. | definitely agree | slightly agree | slightly disagree | definitely disagree |
| 8. | When I'm reading a story, I can easily imagine what the characters might look like. | definitely agree | slightly agree | slightly disagree | definitely disagree |
| 9. | I am fascinated by dates. | definitely agree | slightly agree | slightly disagree | definitely disagree |
| 10. | In a social group, I can easily keep track of several different people's conversations. | definitely agree | slightly agree | slightly disagree | definitely disagree |
| 11. | I find social situations easy. | definitely agree | slightly agree | slightly disagree | definitely disagree |
| 12. | I tend to notice details that others do not. | definitely agree | slightly agree | slightly disagree | definitely disagree |
| 13. | I would rather go to a library than a party. | definitely agree | slightly agree | slightly disagree | definitely disagree |
| 14. | I find making up stories easy. | definitely agree | slightly agree | slightly disagree | definitely disagree |
| 15. | I find myself drawn more strongly to people than to things. | definitely agree | slightly agree | slightly disagree | definitely disagree |
| 16. | I tend to have very strong interests which I get upset about if I can't pursue. | definitely agree | slightly agree | slightly disagree | definitely disagree |
| 17. | I enjoy social chit-chat. | definitely agree | slightly agree | slightly disagree | definitely disagree |
| 18. | When I talk, it isn't always easy for others to get a word in edgeways. | definitely agree | slightly agree | slightly disagree | definitely disagree |

| | |  |  |  |  |
|---|---|---|---|---|---|
| 19. | I am fascinated by numbers. | definitely agree | slightly agree | slightly disagree | definitely disagree |
| 20. | When I'm reading a story, I find it difficult to work out the characters' intentions. | definitely agree | slightly agree | slightly disagree | definitely disagree |
| 21. | I don't particularly enjoy reading fiction. | definitely agree | slightly agree | slightly disagree | definitely disagree |
| 22. | I find it hard to make new friends. | definitely agree | slightly agree | slightly disagree | definitely disagree |
| 23. | I notice patterns in things all the time. | definitely agree | slightly agree | slightly disagree | definitely disagree |
| 24. | I would rather go to the theatre than a museum. | definitely agree | slightly agree | slightly disagree | definitely disagree |
| 25. | It does not upset me if my daily routine is disturbed. | definitely agree | slightly agree | slightly disagree | definitely disagree |
| 26. | I frequently find that I don't know how to keep a conversation going. | definitely agree | slightly agree | slightly disagree | definitely disagree |
| 27. | I find it easy to "read between the lines" when someone is talking to me. | definitely agree | slightly agree | slightly disagree | definitely disagree |
| 28. | I usually concentrate more on the whole picture, rather than the small details. | definitely agree | slightly agree | slightly disagree | definitely disagree |
| 29. | I am not very good at remembering phone numbers. | definitely agree | slightly agree | slightly disagree | definitely disagree |
| 30. | I don't usually notice small changes in a situation, or a person's appearance. | definitely agree | slightly agree | slightly disagree | definitely disagree |

| | |  |  |  |  |
|---|---|---|---|---|---|
| 31. | I know how to tell if someone listening to me is getting bored. | definitely agree | slightly agree | slightly disagree | definitely disagree |
| 32. | I find it easy to do more than one thing at once. | definitely agree | slightly agree | slightly disagree | definitely disagree |
| 33. | When I talk on the phone, I'm not sure when it's my turn to speak. | definitely agree | slightly agree | slightly disagree | definitely disagree |
| 34. | I enjoy doing things spontaneously. | definitely agree | slightly agree | slightly disagree | definitely disagree |
| 35. | I am often the last to understand the point of a joke. | definitely agree | slightly agree | slightly disagree | definitely disagree |
| 36. | I find it easy to work out what someone is thinking or feeling just by looking at their face. | definitely agree | slightly agree | slightly disagree | definitely disagree |
| 37. | If there is an interruption, I can switch back to what I was doing very quickly. | definitely agree | slightly agree | slightly disagree | definitely disagree |
| 38. | I am good at social chit-chat. | definitely agree | slightly agree | slightly disagree | definitely disagree |
| 39. | People often tell me that I keep going on and on about the same thing. | definitely agree | slightly agree | slightly disagree | definitely disagree |
| 40. | When I was young, I used to enjoy playing games involving pretending with other children. | definitely agree | slightly agree | slightly disagree | definitely disagree |

| | definitely agree | slightly agree | slightly disagree | definitely disagree |
|---|---|---|---|---|
| 41. I like to collect information about categories of things (e.g. types of car, types of bird, types of train, types of plant, etc.). | | | | |
| 42. I find it difficult to imagine what it would be like to be someone else. | | | | |
| 43. I like to plan any activities I participate in carefully. | | | | |
| 44. I enjoy social occasions. | | | | |
| 45. I find it difficult to work out people's intentions. | | | | |
| 46. New situations make me anxious. | | | | |
| 47. I enjoy meeting new people. | | | | |
| 48. I am a good diplomat. | | | | |
| 49. I am not very good at remembering people's dates of birth. | | | | |
| 50. I find it very easy to play games with children that involve pretending. | | | | |

## How to score your AQ

Score one point for each of the following items you answered "definitely agree" or "slightly agree:" 2, 4, 5, 6 ,7, 9, 12, 13, 16, 18, 19, 20, 21, 22, 23, 26, 33, 35, 39, 41, 42, 43, 45, 46.

Score one point for each of the following items if you answered "definitely disagree" or "slightly disagree:" 1, 3, 8, 10, 11, 14, 15, 17, 24, 25, 27, 28, 29, 30, 31, 32, 34, 36, 37, 38, 40, 44, 47, 48, 49, 50.

Add up all the points you have scored to obtain your AQ score.

## How to interpret your AQ score

0–10 = You have a low number of autistic traits.

11–22 = You have an average number of autistic traits (most men score about 17 and most women score about 15).

23–31 = You have an above average number of autistic traits.

32–50 = You have a very high number of autistic traits (most people with an autism spectrum condition score about 35).

*Source:* Baron-Cohen *et al.*, 2001, pp.15–16.
Reproduced with permission.

# THE ADULT EMPATHY QUOTIENT (EQ) TEST

Below is a list of statements. Please read each statement carefully and rate how strongly you agree or disagree with it by circling your answer. There are no right or wrong answers. Please answer every question.

| | | | | | |
|---|---|---|---|---|---|
| 1. | I can easily tell if someone else wants to enter a conversation. | strongly agree | slightly agree | slightly disagree | strongly disagree |
| 2. | I prefer animals to humans. | strongly agree | slightly agree | slightly disagree | strongly disagree |
| 3. | I try to keep up with the current trends and fashions. | strongly agree | slightly agree | slightly disagree | strongly disagree |
| 4. | I find it difficult to explain to others things that I understand easily, when they don't understand it first time. | strongly agree | slightly agree | slightly disagree | strongly disagree |
| 5. | I dream most nights. | strongly agree | slightly agree | slightly disagree | strongly disagree |
| 6. | I really enjoy caring for other people. | strongly agree | slightly agree | slightly disagree | strongly disagree |
| 7. | I try to solve my own problems rather than discussing them with others. | strongly agree | slightly agree | slightly disagree | strongly disagree |

| | | strongly agree | slightly agree | slightly disagree | strongly disagree |
|---|---|---|---|---|---|
| 8. | I find it hard to know what to do in a social situation. | strongly agree | slightly agree | slightly disagree | strongly disagree |
| 9. | I am at my best first thing in the morning. | strongly agree | slightly agree | slightly disagree | strongly disagree |
| 10. | People often tell me that I went too far in driving my point home in a discussion. | strongly agree | slightly agree | slightly disagree | strongly disagree |
| 11. | It doesn't bother me too much if I am late meeting a friend. | strongly agree | slightly agree | slightly disagree | strongly disagree |
| 12. | Friendships and relationships are just too difficult, so I tend not to bother with them. | strongly agree | slightly agree | slightly disagree | strongly disagree |
| 13. | I would never break a law, no matter how minor. | strongly agree | slightly agree | slightly disagree | strongly disagree |
| 14. | I often find it difficult to judge if something is rude or polite. | strongly agree | slightly agree | slightly disagree | strongly disagree |
| 15. | In a conversation, I tend to focus on my own thoughts rather than on what my listener might be thinking. | strongly agree | slightly agree | slightly disagree | strongly disagree |
| 16. | I prefer practical jokes to verbal humor. | strongly agree | slightly agree | slightly disagree | strongly disagree |
| 17. | I live life for today rather than the future. | strongly agree | slightly agree | slightly disagree | strongly disagree |
| 18. | When I was a child, I enjoyed cutting up worms to see what would happen. | strongly agree | slightly agree | slightly disagree | strongly disagree |
| 19. | I can pick up quickly if someone says one thing but means another. | strongly agree | slightly agree | slightly disagree | strongly disagree |

| | | strongly agree | slightly agree | slightly disagree | strongly disagree |
|---|---|---|---|---|---|
| 20. | I tend to have very strong opinions about morality. | strongly agree | slightly agree | slightly disagree | strongly disagree |
| 21. | It is hard for me to see why some things upset people so much. | strongly agree | slightly agree | slightly disagree | strongly disagree |
| 22. | I find it easy to put myself in somebody else's shoes. | strongly agree | slightly agree | slightly disagree | strongly disagree |
| 23. | I think that good manners are the most important thing a parent can teach their child. | strongly agree | slightly agree | slightly disagree | strongly disagree |
| 24. | I like to do things on the spur of the moment. | strongly agree | slightly agree | slightly disagree | strongly disagree |
| 25. | I am good at predicting how someone will feel. | strongly agree | slightly agree | slightly disagree | strongly disagree |
| 26. | I am quick to spot when someone in a group is feeling awkward or uncomfortable. | strongly agree | slightly agree | slightly disagree | strongly disagree |
| 27. | If I say something that someone else is offended by, I think that that's their problem, not mine. | strongly agree | slightly agree | slightly disagree | strongly disagree |
| 28. | If anyone asked me if I liked their haircut, I would reply truthfully, even if I didn't like it. | strongly agree | slightly agree | slightly disagree | strongly disagree |
| 29. | I can't always see why someone should have felt offended by a remark. | strongly agree | slightly agree | slightly disagree | strongly disagree |
| 30. | People often tell me that I am very unpredictable. | strongly agree | slightly agree | slightly disagree | strongly disagree |
| 31. | I enjoy being the centre of attention at any social gathering. | strongly agree | slightly agree | slightly disagree | strongly disagree |

| | | strongly agree | slightly agree | slightly disagree | strongly disagree |
|---|---|---|---|---|---|
| 32. | Seeing people cry doesn't really upset me. | strongly agree | slightly agree | slightly disagree | strongly disagree |
| 33. | I enjoy having discussions about politics. | strongly agree | slightly agree | slightly disagree | strongly disagree |
| 34. | I am very blunt, which some people take to be rudeness, even though this is unintentional. | strongly agree | slightly agree | slightly disagree | strongly disagree |
| 35. | I don't tend to find social situations confusing. | strongly agree | slightly agree | slightly disagree | strongly disagree |
| 36. | Other people tell me I am good at understanding how they are feeling and what they are thinking. | strongly agree | slightly agree | slightly disagree | strongly disagree |
| 37. | When I talk to people, I tend to talk about their experiences rather than my own. | strongly agree | slightly agree | slightly disagree | strongly disagree |
| 38. | It upsets me to see an animal in pain. | strongly agree | slightly agree | slightly disagree | strongly disagree |
| 39. | I am able to make decisions without being influenced by people's feelings. | strongly agree | slightly agree | slightly disagree | strongly disagree |
| 40. | I can't relax until I have done everything I had planned to do that day. | strongly agree | slightly agree | slightly disagree | strongly disagree |
| 41. | I can easily tell if someone else is interested or bored with what I am saying. | strongly agree | slightly agree | slightly disagree | strongly disagree |
| 42. | I get upset if I see people suffering on news programs. | strongly agree | slightly agree | slightly disagree | strongly disagree |

| | | strongly agree | slightly agree | slightly disagree | strongly disagree |
|---|---|---|---|---|---|
| 43. | Friends usually talk to me about their problems as they say that I am very understanding. | strongly agree | slightly agree | slightly disagree | strongly disagree |
| 44. | I can sense if I am intruding, even if the other person doesn't tell me. | strongly agree | slightly agree | slightly disagree | strongly disagree |
| 45. | I often start new hobbies but quickly become bored with them and move on to something else. | strongly agree | slightly agree | slightly disagree | strongly disagree |
| 46. | People sometimes tell me that I have gone too far with teasing. | strongly agree | slightly agree | slightly disagree | strongly disagree |
| 47. | I would be too nervous to go on a big rollercoaster. | strongly agree | slightly agree | slightly disagree | strongly disagree |
| 48. | Other people often say that I am insensitive, though I don't always see why. | strongly agree | slightly agree | slightly disagree | strongly disagree |
| 49. | If I see a stranger in a group, I think that it is up to them to make an effort to join in. | strongly agree | slightly agree | slightly disagree | strongly disagree |
| 50. | I usually stay emotionally detached when watching a film. | strongly agree | slightly agree | slightly disagree | strongly disagree |
| 51. | I like to be very organized in day-to-day life and often make lists of the chores I have to do. | strongly agree | slightly agree | slightly disagree | strongly disagree |
| 52. | I can tune into how someone else feels rapidly and intuitively. | strongly agree | slightly agree | slightly disagree | strongly disagree |
| 53. | I don't like to take risks. | strongly agree | slightly agree | slightly disagree | strongly disagree |

| | | strongly agree | slightly agree | slightly disagree | strongly disagree |
|---|---|---|---|---|---|
| 54. | I can easily work out what another person might want to talk about. | strongly agree | slightly agree | slightly disagree | strongly disagree |
| 55. | I can tell if someone is masking their true emotion. | strongly agree | slightly agree | slightly disagree | strongly disagree |
| 56. | Before making a decision I always weigh up the pros and cons. | strongly agree | slightly agree | slightly disagree | strongly disagree |
| 57. | I don't consciously work out the rules of social situations. | strongly agree | slightly agree | slightly disagree | strongly disagree |
| 58. | I am good at predicting what someone will do. | strongly agree | slightly agree | slightly disagree | strongly disagree |
| 59. | I tend to get emotionally involved with a friend's problems. | strongly agree | slightly agree | slightly disagree | strongly disagree |
| 60. | I can usually appreciate the other person's viewpoint, even if I don't agree with it. | strongly agree | slightly agree | slightly disagree | strongly disagree |

## How to score your EQ

Score two points for each of the following items if you answered "strongly agree" or one point if you answered "slightly agree:" 1, 6, 19, 22, 25, 26, 35, 36, 37, 38, 41, 42, 43, 44, 52, 54, 55, 57, 58, 59, 60.

Score two points for each of the following items if you answered "strongly disagree" or one point if you answered "slightly disagree:" 4, 8, 10, 11, 12, 14, 15, 18, 21, 27, 28, 29, 32, 34, 39, 46, 48, 49, 50.

The other items are not scored. Add up all the points you have scored to obtain your EQ.

## How to interpret your EQ score

On average, most women score about 47 and most men about 42. Most people on the autism spectrum score about 20.

0–32 = You have a lower than average ability for understanding how other people feel and responding appropriately.

33–52 = You have an average ability for understanding how other people feel and responding appropriately.

53–63 = You have an above average ability for understanding how other people feel and responding appropriately.

64–80 = You have a very high ability for understanding how other people feel and responding appropriately.

*Source:* Baron-Cohen, S., and Wheelwright, S. (2004) pp. 171–173. Reproduced with permission.

# THE ADULT SYSTEMIZING QUOTIENT (SQ) TEST

Below is a list of statements. Please read each statement carefully and rate how strongly you agree or disagree with it by circling your answer. There are no right or wrong answers. Please answer every question.

| | | |
|---|---|---|
| 1. When I listen to a piece of music, I always notice the way it's structured. | strongly agree | slightly agree | slightly disagree | strongly disagree |
| 2. I adhere to common superstitions. | strongly agree | slightly agree | slightly disagree | strongly disagree |
| 3. I often make resolutions, but find it hard to stick to them. | strongly agree | slightly agree | slightly disagree | strongly disagree |
| 4. I prefer to read non-fiction than fiction. | strongly agree | slightly agree | slightly disagree | strongly disagree |
| 5. If I were buying a car, I would want to obtain specific information about its engine capacity. | strongly agree | slightly agree | slightly disagree | strongly disagree |
| 6. When I look at a painting, I do not usually think about the technique involved in making it. | strongly agree | slightly agree | slightly disagree | strongly disagree |

7. If there was a problem with the electrical wiring in my home, I'd be able to fix it myself.

strongly agree　slightly agree　slightly disagree　strongly disagree

8. When I have a dream, I find it difficult to remember precise details about the dream the next day.

strongly agree　slightly agree　slightly disagree　strongly disagree

9. When I watch a film, I prefer to be with a group of friends, rather than alone.

strongly agree　slightly agree　slightly disagree　strongly disagree

10. I am interested in learning about different religions.

strongly agree　slightly agree　slightly disagree　strongly disagree

11. I rarely read articles or web pages about new technology.

strongly agree　slightly agree　slightly disagree　strongly disagree

12. I do not enjoy games that involve a high degree of strategy.

strongly agree　slightly agree　slightly disagree　strongly disagree

13. I am fascinated by how machines work.

strongly agree　slightly agree　slightly disagree　strongly disagree

14. I make a point of listening to the news each morning.

strongly agree　slightly agree　slightly disagree　strongly disagree

15. In math, I am intrigued by the rules and patterns governing numbers.

strongly agree　slightly agree　slightly disagree　strongly disagree

16. I am bad about keeping in touch with old friends.

strongly agree　slightly agree　slightly disagree　strongly disagree

17. When I am relating a story, I often leave out details and just give the gist of what happened.

strongly agree　slightly agree　slightly disagree　strongly disagree

| | | | | |
|---|---|---|---|---|
| 18. | I find it difficult to understand instruction manuals for putting appliances together. | strongly agree | slightly agree | slightly disagree | strongly disagree |

| | | | | |
|---|---|---|---|---|
| 19. | When I look at an animal, I like to know the precise species it belongs to. | strongly agree | slightly agree | slightly disagree | strongly disagree |

| | | | | |
|---|---|---|---|---|
| 20. | If I were buying a computer, I would want to know exact details about its hard drive capacity and processor speed. | strongly agree | slightly agree | slightly disagree | strongly disagree |

| | | | | |
|---|---|---|---|---|
| 21. | I enjoy participating in sports. | strongly agree | slightly agree | slightly disagree | strongly disagree |

| | | | | |
|---|---|---|---|---|
| 22. | I try to avoid doing household chores if I can. | strongly agree | slightly agree | slightly disagree | strongly disagree |

| | | | | |
|---|---|---|---|---|
| 23. | When I cook, I do not think about exactly how different methods and ingredients contribute to the final product. | strongly agree | slightly agree | slightly disagree | strongly disagree |

| | | | | |
|---|---|---|---|---|
| 24. | I find it difficult to read and understand maps. | strongly agree | slightly agree | slightly disagree | strongly disagree |

| | | | | |
|---|---|---|---|---|
| 25. | If I had a collection (e.g. CDs, coins, stamps), it would be highly organized. | strongly agree | slightly agree | slightly disagree | strongly disagree |

| | | | | |
|---|---|---|---|---|
| 26. | When I look at a piece of furniture, I do not notice the details of how it was constructed. | strongly agree | slightly agree | slightly disagree | strongly disagree |

| | | | | |
|---|---|---|---|---|
| 27. | The idea of engaging in "risk-taking" activities appeals to me. | strongly agree | slightly agree | slightly disagree | strongly disagree |

| | | | | |
|---|---|---|---|---|
| 28. | When I learn about historical events, I do not focus on exact dates. | strongly agree | slightly agree | slightly disagree | strongly disagree |

| | | strongly agree | slightly agree | slightly disagree | strongly disagree |
|---|---|---|---|---|---|
| 29. | When I read the newspaper, I am drawn to tables of information, such as football scores or stock market indices. | strongly agree | slightly agree | slightly disagree | strongly disagree |
| 30. | When I learn a language, I become intrigued by its grammatical rules. | strongly agree | slightly agree | slightly disagree | strongly disagree |
| 31. | I find it difficult to learn my way around a new city. | strongly agree | slightly agree | slightly disagree | strongly disagree |
| 32. | I do not tend to watch science documentaries on television or read articles about science and nature. | strongly agree | slightly agree | slightly disagree | strongly disagree |
| 33. | If I were buying a stereo, I would want to know about its precise technical features. | strongly agree | slightly agree | slightly disagree | strongly disagree |
| 34. | I find it easy to grasp exactly how odds work in betting. | strongly agree | slightly agree | slightly disagree | strongly disagree |
| 35. | I am not very meticulous when I carry out do-it-yourself projects. | strongly agree | slightly agree | slightly disagree | strongly disagree |
| 36. | I find it easy to carry on a conversation with someone I've just met. | strongly agree | slightly agree | slightly disagree | strongly disagree |
| 37. | When I look at a building, I am curious about the precise way it was constructed. | strongly agree | slightly agree | slightly disagree | strongly disagree |
| 38. | When an election is being held, I am not interested in the results for each constituency. | strongly agree | slightly agree | slightly disagree | strongly disagree |

| | | strongly agree | slightly agree | slightly disagree | strongly disagree |
|---|---|---|---|---|---|
| 39. | When I lend someone money, I expect them to pay me back exactly what they owe me. | | | | |
| 40. | I find it difficult to understand information the bank sends me on different investment and saving systems. | | | | |
| 41. | When traveling by train, I often wonder exactly how the rail networks are coordinated. | | | | |
| 42. | When I buy a new appliance, I do not read the instruction manual very thoroughly. | | | | |
| 43. | If I were buying a camera, I would not look carefully into the quality of the lens. | | | | |
| 44. | When I read something, I always notice whether it is grammatically correct. | | | | |
| 45. | When I hear the weather forecast, I am not very interested in the meteorological patterns. | | | | |
| 46. | I often wonder what it would be like to be someone else. | | | | |
| 47. | I find it difficult to do two things at once. | | | | |
| 48. | When I look at a mountain, I think about how precisely it was formed. | | | | |
| 49. | I can easily visualize how the freeways in my region link up. | | | | |

| | | | | |
|---|---|---|---|---|
| 50. When I'm in a restaurant, I often have a hard time deciding what to order. | strongly agree | slightly agree | slightly disagree | strongly disagree |
| 51. When I'm in a plane, I do not think about the aerodynamics. | strongly agree | slightly agree | slightly disagree | strongly disagree |
| 52. I often forget the precise details of conversations I've had. | strongly agree | slightly agree | slightly disagree | strongly disagree |
| 53. When I am walking in the country, I am curious about how the various kinds of trees differ. | strongly agree | slightly agree | slightly disagree | strongly disagree |
| 54. After meeting someone just once or twice, I find it difficult to remember precisely what they look like. | strongly agree | slightly agree | slightly disagree | strongly disagree |
| 55. I am interested in knowing the path a river takes from its source to the sea. | strongly agree | slightly agree | slightly disagree | strongly disagree |
| 56. I do not read legal documents very carefully. | strongly agree | slightly agree | slightly disagree | strongly disagree |
| 57. I am not interested in understanding how wireless communication works. | strongly agree | slightly agree | slightly disagree | strongly disagree |
| 58. I am curious about life on other planets. | strongly agree | slightly agree | slightly disagree | strongly disagree |
| 59. When I travel, I like to learn specific details about the culture of the place I am visiting. | strongly agree | slightly agree | slightly disagree | strongly disagree |
| 60. I do not care to know the names of the plants I see. | strongly agree | slightly agree | slightly disagree | strongly disagree |

## How to score your SQ

Score two points for each of the following items if you answered "strongly agree" or one point if you answered "slightly agree:" 1, 4, 5, 7, 13, 15, 19, 20, 25, 29, 30, 33, 34, 37, 41, 44, 48, 49, 53, 55.

Score two points for each of the following items if you answered "strongly disagree" or one point if you answered "slightly disagree:" 6, 11, 12, 18, 23, 24, 26, 28, 31, 32, 35, 38, 40, 42, 43, 45, 51, 56, 57, 60.

The other items are not scored. Add up all the points you have scored to obtain your SQ.

## How to interpret your SQ score

On average, women score about 24 and men score about 30.

0–19 = You have a lower than average ability for analyzing and exploring a system.

20–39 = You have an average ability for analyzing and exploring a system.

40–50 = You have an above average ability for analyzing and exploring a system.

51–80 = You have a very high ability for analyzing and exploring a system. Three times as many people with an autism spectrum condition fall in this range, compared to typical men, and very few women score this high.

*Source:* Baron-Cohen, S., *et al.*, (2004), pp. 176–179.
Reproduced with permission.

# ABC WORKSHEET

| A = Activating event | B = Belief/ thought | C = Consequence feeling/emotion |
|---|---|---|
|  |  |  |
|  |  |  |
|  |  |  |
|  |  |  |

What was the event or situation?

What thoughts or beliefs did you have about the situation?

How true did that belief seem where 0 percent is not true at all and 100 percent is absolutely true?

How did you feel when the event situation happened?

How did you act?

How did others respond?

# THOUGHT–FEELING WORKSHEET

| THOUGHT:<br>I think… | FEELING:<br>Therefore, I feel… |
|---|---|
|  |  |
|  |  |
|  |  |
|  |  |
|  |  |

# UNHELPFUL THINKING HABITS RECORD FORM

| Demand thinking | Alternative thought |
|---|---|
| Mind reading | Alternative thought |
| All-or-nothing thinking | Alternative thought |
| Emotional reasoning | Alternative thought |

| Overgeneralizing | Alternative thought |
|---|---|
| Labeling | Alternative thought |
| Discounting the positive | Alternative thought |
| Personalizing | Alternative thought |
| Mental filtering | Alternative thought |
| Awfulizing | Alternative thought |

# CBT SELF-HELP THOUGHT RECORD FORM

| A—Activating events (or experiences) | B—Beliefs about your activating events | C— Consequences of your beliefs |
|---|---|---|
| | Irrational beliefs/ unhelpful automatic thoughts | Inappropriate emotional consequences |
| | Rational alternative beliefs | Appropriate emotional consequence |

| D—Disputing/debating your irrational beliefs |
|---|
| 1. Is this thought a fact or my opinion? |
| 2. Do I have evidence to support this? |
| 3. Do I have evidence against this? |
| 4. Is there another, more realistic, way of looking at the situation? |
| 5. Is it really true that I must, should, or have to…? |
| 6. Can I stand it? How have I tolerated these situations in the past? |
| 7. Is this situation really in my control? Is there another explanation other than blaming myself? |
| 8. Am I overgeneralizing from a specific event or occurrence? |
| 9. What's the worst that could realistically happen? How bad would that be? |
| 10. What is a more balanced (rational) alternative belief/thought? |

# DAILY MOOD AND THOUGHT WORKSHEET

| Week # | Mood | Intensity (0–10) | Events | Thoughts |
|---|---|---|---|---|
| Mon | | | | |
| Tues | | | | |
| Wed | | | | |
| Thurs | | | | |
| Fri | | | | |
| Sat | | | | |
| Sun | | | | |

# SELF-TALK RECORD FORM

| Situation | Negative self-talk | Positive self-talk |
|-----------|--------------------|--------------------|
|           |                    |                    |
|           |                    |                    |
|           |                    |                    |
|           |                    |                    |

# COPING THOUGHT WORKSHEET

| Distressing event or situation | Coping thought |
|---|---|
| | |
| | |
| | |
| | |
| | |

# PROBLEM-SOLVING WORKSHEET

---

1. **Problem identification:** What is the concern?

---

2. **Goal selection:** What do I want to achieve?

---

3. **Alternatives:** What can I do? List the pros and cons (brainstorming).

---

4. **Consider the consequences:** What might happen? Positive and negative effects?

5. **Decision-making:** What is my decision? Choose one possible solution.

6. **Implementation:** Now do it! Carry out your plan/solution.

7. **Evaluation:** Did it work? If not, make adjustments or return to steps 3 and 4.

# MAINTAINING CHANGE WORKSHEET

---

**What have I learned from CBT?**



---

**What was most helpful?**



---

**What can I do to prevent a setback?**



---

**What are my high-risk situations of this happening?**



---

**What events/situations/triggers cause me to be more vulnerable?**



---

What are the signs? Red flags?
Thoughts/feelings/behaviors?

What can I do to avoid losing emotional control?
What could I do differently? What would work best?
When I'm struggling or feeling bad, what could I do that
will help?

What could I do if I did lose emotional control?
What has helped? What have I learned? Who can help?

# UNHELPFUL THINKING HABITS

1. *Demand thinking—"Shoulds, musts, and ought tos"*

2. *All or Nothing Thinking—or Black and White thinking*

3. *Overgeneralizing—Seeing a pattern based on a single event*

4. *Discounting the Positive—Minimizing positive experiences*

5. *Mental Filtering—Focusing on the negative and ignoring the positive*

6. *Mind Reading or Jumping to Conclusions—Assuming you know what others think*

7. *Emotional Reasoning—Confusing fact with feeling*

8. *Labeling—Assigning labels to ourselves and others*

9. *Personalizing—Blaming yourself and assuming responsibility for negative events*

10. *Catastrophizing or Awfulizing—Imagining the worse case scenario*

# MAJOR IRRATIONAL IDEAS/BELIEFS

1.  *You must—yes, must—have sincere love and approval almost all of the time from people you find significant.*

2.  *You must prove yourself thoroughly competent, adequate, and achieving at all times, or you must at least have real competence or talent in some important area.*

3.  *You have to view life as awful, terrible, horrible, or catastrophic when you get seriously frustrated, treated unfairly, or rejected.*

4.  *People who harm you or behave badly or unfairly should be severely blamed, reprimanded, and punished for their behavior. They are bad and terrible individuals.*

5.  *If something seems dangerous or fearsome, you must become terribly occupied with it and upset about it.*

6.  *People and things should turn out better than they do and you have to view it as awful and horrible if you do not find perfect solutions to life's hassles.*

7.  *Emotional misery comes from external pressure and you have little ability to control your feelings or rid yourself of anxiety, depression, and hostility.*

8.  *You will find it easier to avoid facing many of life's difficulties and self-responsibilities than to undertake more rewarding forms of self-discipline.*

9. *Your past remains all-important and because something once strongly influenced your life, it has to keep determining your feelings and behavior today.*

10. *You achieve happiness by inertia and inaction or by passively and noncommittally enjoying yourself.*

# REFERENCES

American Psychiatric Association (2013) *Diagnostic and Statistical Manual of Mental Disorders* (fifth edition). Washington, DC: APA.

Anderson, K. A., Shattuck, P. T., Cooper, B. P., Roux, A. M., and Wagner, M. (2014) 'Prevalence and correlates of postsecondary residential status among young adults with an autism spectrum disorder.' *Autism*, 18, 562–570. doi: 10.1177/1362361313481860

Attwood, T. (2004) 'Cognitive behaviour therapy for children and adults with Asperger's syndrome.' *Behaviour Change, 21*, 147–162.

Attwood, T. (2006) *The Complete Guide to Asperger's Syndrome*. London, UK: Jessica Kingsley Publishers.

Baron-Cohen, S. (1995) *Mindblindness: An Essay on Autism and Theory of Mind*. Cambridge, MA: MIT Press/Bradford Books.

Baron-Cohen, S. (2004) *The Essential Difference: Male and Female Brains and the Truth about Autism*. New York, NY: Basic Books.

Baron-Cohen, S. (2008) *Autism and Asperger Syndrome: The Facts*. New York, NY: Oxford University Press.

Baron-Cohen, S., Richler, J., Bisarya, D., Gurunathan, N., and Wheelwright, S. (2004) 'The Systemizing Quotient: An Investigation of Adults with Asperger Syndrome or High-Functioning Autism, and Normal Sex Differences.' In U. Frith and E. Hill (eds) *Autism: Mind and Brain*. New York, NY: Oxford University Press.

Baron-Cohen, S., and Wheelwright, S. (2004) 'The Empathy Quotient (EQ): An investigation of adults with Asperger Syndrome and high-functioning autism, and normal sex differences.' *Journal of Autism and Developmental Disorders, 34*, 163–175.

Baron-Cohen, S., Wheelwright, S., Lawson, J., Griffin, R., Ashwin, C., Billington, J., and Chakrabarti, B. (2005) 'Empathizing and Systemizing in Autism Spectrum Conditions.' In F. R. Volkmar, R. Paul, A. Klin, and D. Cohen (eds.) *Handbook of Autism and Pervasive Developmental Disorders, Volume 1: Diagnosis, Development, Neurobiology, and Behavior* (third edition). Hoboken, NJ: Wiley.

Baron-Cohen, S., Wheelwright, R., Skinner, J., Martin, J. and Clubley, E. (2001) 'The Autism Spectrum Quotient (AQ): Evidence from Asperger syndrome/ high functioning autism, males and females, scientists and mathematicians.' *Journal of Autism and Developmental Disorders, 31*, 5–17.

Beck, J. S. (1995) *Cognitive Therapy: Basics and Beyond.* New York, NY: Guilford Press.

Beck, A. T., Rush, A. J., Shaw, B. F., and Emery, G. (1979) *Cognitive Therapy of Depression.* New York, NY: Guilford Press.

Cardaciotto L., and Herbert J. (2004) 'Cognitive behavior therapy for social anxiety disorder in the context of Asperger's syndrome: A single-subject report.' *Cognitive and Behavioral Practice, 11*, 75–81.

Constantino, J. N., and Todd, R. D. (2003) 'Autistic traits in the general population: A twin study.' *Archives of General Psychiatry, 60*, 524–530.

Cully, J. A., and Teten, A. L. (2008) *A Therapist's Guide to Brief Cognitive Behavioral Therapy.* Department of Veterans Affairs South Central MIRECC, Houston. Available at www.mirecc.va.gov/visn16/docs/therapists_guide_to_brief_cbtmanual.pdf, accessed 11th August 2014.

DeRubeis, R. J., Webb, C. A., Tang, T. Z., and Beck, A. T. (2010) 'Cognitive Therapy.' In K. S. Dobson (ed.) *Handbook of Cognitive Behavioral Therapies* (third edition). New York, NY: Guilford.

Dobson, K. S., and Dozois, D. J. A. (2010) 'Historical and Philosophical Bases of the Cognitive-behavioral Therapies.' In K. S. Dobson (ed.) *Handbook of Cognitive Behavioral Therapies* (third edition). New York, NY: Guilford.

Dryden, W., David, D., and Ellis, A. (2010) 'Rational Emotive Behavior Therapy.' In K. S. Dobson (ed.) *Handbook of Cognitive Behavioral Therapies* (third edition). New York, NY: Guilford.

Dryden, W. and DiGiuseppe, R. (1990) *A Primer on Rational-Emotive Therapy.* Champaign, IL: Research Press.

D'Zurilla, T. J., and Nezu, A. M., (2010) 'Problem-Solving Therapy.' In K. S. Dobson (ed.) *Handbook of Cognitive Behavioral Therapies* (third edition). New York, NY: Guilford.

Ellis, A. (1988) *How to Stubbornly Refuse to Make Yourself Miserable about Anything— Yes Anything!* Secaucus, NJ: Lyle Stuart, Inc.

Ellis, A., and Dryden, W. (1987) *The Practice of Rational Emotive Therapy.* New York, NY: Springer.

Ellis, A., and Dryden, W. (2007) *The Practice of Rational Emotive Behavior Therapy* (second edition). New York, NY: Springer Publishing.

Ellis, A., and Harper, R. A. (1975) *A New Guide to Rational Living.* N. Hollywood, CA: Wilshire Book Company.

Epp, A. M., and Dobson, K. S. (2010) 'The Evidence Base For Cognitive-Behavioral Therapy.' In K. S. Dobson (ed.) *Handbook of Cognitive Behavioral Therapies* (third edition). New York, NY: Guilford.

Frith, U. (1989) *Autism: Explaining the Enigma*. Oxford, UK: Blackwell.

Fruzzetti, A. E., and Erikson, K. R. (2010) 'Mindfulness and Acceptance Interventions in Cognitive-Behavioral Therapy.' In K. S. Dobson (ed.) *Handbook of Cognitive Behavioral Therapies* (third edition). New York, NY: Guilford.

Gaus, V. L. (2007) *Cognitive-Behavioral Therapy for Adult Asperger Syndrome*. New York, NY: Guilford Press.

Gaus, V. L. (2011) 'Adult Asperger syndrome and the utility of cognitive behavioral therapy.' *Journal of Contemporary Psychotherapy, 41*, 47–56.

Ghaziuddin, M., Ghaziuddin N., and Greden J. (2002) 'Depression in persons with autism: Implications for research and clinical care.' *Journal of Autism and Developmental Disorders, 32*, 299–306.

Grandin, T., and Barron, S. (2005) *Unwritten Rules of Social Relationships: Decoding Social Mysteries through the Unique Perspectives of Autism*. Arlington, TX: Future Horizons, Inc.

Happé, F. (2005) 'The weak central coherence account of autism.' In F. R. Volkmar, R. Paul, A. Klin, and D. Cohen (eds.) *Handbook of Autism and Pervasive Developmental Disorders, Volume 1: Diagnosis, Development, Neurobiology, and Behavior* (third edition). Hoboken, NJ: Wiley.

Hare, D. J. (1997) 'The use of cognitive-behaviour therapy with people with Asperger's syndrome.' *Autism, 1*, 215–225.

Hauck, P. A. (1980) *Brief Counseling with RET*. Philadelphia, PA: Westminster Press.

Holmboe, K., Rijsdijk, F. V., Hallett, V., Happ, F., Plomin, R., and Ronald, A. (2014) 'Strong genetic influences on the stability of autistic traits in childhood.' *Journal of the American Academy of Child & Adolescent Psychiatry*, 53, 2, 221–230. doi: 10.1016/j.jaac.2013.11.001

Horder, J., Wilson, C. E., Mendez, M. A., and Murphy, D. G. (2014) 'Autistic traits and abnormal sensory experiences in adults.' *Journal of Autism and Developmental Disorders*, 44, 1461–1469. doi: 10.1007/s10803-013-2012-7

Howlin, P. A. (2000) 'Outcome in adult life for more able individuals with Asperger syndrome.' *Autism, 4*, 63–83.

Howlin, P. (2005) 'Outcomes in Autism Spectrum Disorders.' In F. R. Volkmar, R. Paul, A. Klin, and D. Cohen (eds). *Handbook of Autism and Pervasive Developmental Disorders, Volume 1: Diagnosis, Development, Neurobiology, and Behavior* (third edition). Hoboken, NJ: Wiley.

Joshi G., Wozniak J., Petty, C., Martelon, M. K., Fried, R., Bolfek, A., and Biederman J. (2013) 'Psychiatric comorbidity and functioning in a clinically referred population of adults with autism spectrum disorders: a comparative study.' *Journal of Autism and Developmental Disorders, 43*, 1314–1325. doi: 10.1007/s10803–012–1679–5

Luke, L., Clare, I. C. H., Ring, H., Redley, M., and Watson, P. (2012) 'Decision-making difficulties experienced by adults with autism spectrum conditions.' *Autism*, 16, 612–621.

Mazurek, M. O. (2014) 'Loneliness, friendship, and well-being in adults with autism spectrum disorders.' *Autism*, 18, 223–232. doi: 10.1177/1362361312474121

Mazurek, M. O., Kanne, S. M., and Wodka, E. L. (2013) 'Physical aggression in children and adolescents with autism spectrum disorders.' *Research in Autism Spectrum Disorders*, 7, 455–465.

Mazzone, L., Ruta, L., and Reale, L. (2012) 'Psychiatric comorbidities in Asperger syndrome and high functioning autism: Diagnostic challenges.' *Annals of General Psychiatry*, *11*, 16, doi:10.1186/1744–859X–11–16, available at www.annals-general-psychiatry.com/content/pdf/1744-859X-11-16.pdf, accessed 13 October 2014.

Orsmond, G. I., Shattuck, P. T., Cooper, B. P., Sterzing, P. R., and Anderson, K. A. (2013) 'Social participation among young adults with an autism spectrum disorder.' *Journal of Autism and Developmental Disorders*, 43, 2710–2719. doi: 10.1007/s10803-013-1833-8

Ozsivadjian, A., Knott, F., and Magiati, I. (2012) 'Parent and child perspectives on the nature of anxiety in children and young people with autism spectrum disorders: A focus group study.' *Autism*, 16, 107–121. doi: 10.1177/1362361311431703

Scattone, D., and Mong, M. (2013) 'Cognitive behavior therapy in the treatment of anxiety for adolescents and adults with autism spectrum disorders.' *Psychology in the Schools*, *50*, 923–935.

Seltzer, M. M., Shattuck P., Abbeduto L., et al., (2004) 'Trajectory of development in adolescents and adults with autism.' *Mental Retardation and Developmental Disabilities Research Reviews*, 10, 234–247.

Shea, V., and Mesibov, G. B. (2005) 'Adolescents and Adults with Autism.' In F. R. Volkmar, R. Paul, A. Klin, and D. Cohen (eds) *Handbook of Autism and Pervasive Developmental Disorders, Vol. 1: Diagnosis, Development, Neurobiology, and Behavior* (third edition). Hoboken, NJ: Wiley.

Sterling, L., Dawson, G., Estes A., et al., (2008) 'Characteristics associated with presence of depressive symptoms in adults with autism spectrum disorder.' *Journal of Autism and Developmental Disorders*, *38*, 1011–1018.

Tavassoli, T., Miller, L. J., Schoen, S. A., Nielsen, D. M., and Baron-Cohen, S. (2014) 'Sensory over-responsivity in adults with autism spectrum conditions.' *Autism*, 18, 428–432. doi: 10.1177/1362361313477246

Vivyan, C. (2013) *An Introductory Self-Help Course in Cognitive-Behavioural Therapy.* Available at www.getselfhelp.co.uk/docs/SelfHelpCourse.pdf, accessed 15 October 2014.

Walen, S. R., DiGiuseppe, R., and Wessler, R. L. (1980) *A Practitioner's Guide to Rational-Emotive Therapy.* New York, NY: Oxford University Press.

Wilkinson, L. A. (2007) 'Adults with Asperger syndrome: A lost generation?' *Autism Spectrum Quarterly*, Summer, 15–18.

Wilkinson, L. A. (2008) 'Adults with Asperger syndrome: A childhood disorder grows up.' *The Psychologist, 21,* 764–770.

Wilkinson, L. A. (2011) 'Mindblindness.' In S. Goldstein and J. Naglieri (eds) *Encyclopedia of Child Behavior and Development,* Part 13. New York, NY: Springer-Verlag.

# ABOUT THE AUTHOR

**Lee A. Wilkinson, PhD, CCBT** is an applied researcher and practitioner. He is a nationally certified and licensed school psychologist, chartered psychologist, registered practitioner psychologist, and certified cognitive behavioral therapist. Dr. Wilkinson practices in Florida where he provides consultation services for individuals, families and professionals on a wide variety of topics related to autism spectrum conditions. He is also a university educator and serves on the school psychology faculty at Nova Southeastern University and Capella University. His research and professional writing has focused primarily on behavioral consultation and therapy, and children and adults with Asperger syndrome and high-functioning autism spectrum conditions. He has published numerous journal articles on these topics both in the US and internationally, and has been invited as an ad hoc reviewer for peer-reviewed journals such as the *Journal of Remedial and Special Education, Journal of Child Psychology and Psychiatry, Learning and Individual Differences,* and *Autism: The International Journal of Research and Practice.* Dr. Wilkinson is the author of the award-winning book, *A Best Practice Guide to Assessment and Intervention for Autism and Asperger Syndrome in Schools,* published by Jessica Kingsley Publishers. He is also the editor of a new volume in the American Psychological Association (APA) School Psychology Book Series, *Autism Spectrum Disorders in Children and Adolescents: Evidence-Based Assessment and Intervention in Schools.*

# INDEX